CANDLE
BIBLE
QUIZ

Text compiled by Tim Dowley and Deborah Lock

Published by **Candle Books**
www.lionhudson.com
Part of the SPCK Group
SPCK, 36 Causton Street, London, SW1P 4ST

ISBN 978 1 78128 411 7
First edition 2023

Acknowledgments

Scripture quotations taken from the Holy Bible, New International Version, copyright © 1973, 1978, 1984 by the International Bible Society. Used by permission of Zondervan and Hodder & Stoughton Limited.

All rights reserved. The "NIV" and "New International Version" trademarks are registered in the United States Patent and Trademark Office by International Bible Society. Use of either trademark requires the permission of International Bible Society. UK trademark number 1448790.

Picture acknowledgements

Every effort has been made to contact the illustrators of this work, although this has not been possible in all cases. If notified, the publisher will rectify any errors or omissions at the earliest opportunity.

Illustrations
Alan Parry/© Bill Noller International Publishing, San Dimas, CA. 91773 pp. 6, 26, 43, 49, 50, 54, 58, 62, 69, 70, 85, 95, 107, 109, 110, 115, 117, 119, 123, 124
Ann Baum pp. 53, 61
Bill Corbett cover, pp. 3, 11, 14
Bob Moulder p. 68
Donald Harley p. 55
Fred Apps pp. 7, 8, 15, 71
Getty pp. 23 **BibleArtLibrary**, 52, 111 **BibleArtLibrary**, 121
Martin Bustamente pp. 34, 36, 37, 39
Pamela Goodchild p. 122
Peter Dennis pp. 24, 29, 44, 45, 63, 89
Richard Scott pp. 5, 9, 10, 12, 13, 16, 17, 18, 20, 21, 22, 25, 27, 28, 31, 40, 41, 42, 47, 51, 56, 59, 64, 65, 66, 67, 72, 73, 74, 75, 77, 79, 80, 81, 82, 83, 84, 86, 87, 88, 90, 92, 93, 96, 97, 98, 99, 100, 101, 104, 105, 108, 114, 116, 118, 125, 126
Tony Morris pp. 46, 94, 103, 106, 113, 120, 128

Photographs
Dreamstime 35 Gilad Levy
Getty pp. 32, 33 Catalin Daniel Ciolca, 35 Ynot2, 48 gjohnstonphoto,
Tim Dowley Associates p. 57

A catalogue record for this book is available from the British Library

Printed and bound in China, February 2023, LH54

CANDLE
BIBLE
QUIZ

CANDLE
BOOKS

CONTENTS

Bible people

Bible relationships

Bible places

Bible books and verses

Bible times

Old Testament events

CONTENTS

Name the character

1. He anointed King David.

2. She helped her mother-in-law, Naomi.

3. She escaped the city of Sodom but was turned into a pillar of salt.

4. He soothed King Saul by playing the harp.

5. He was the first Christian martyr.

6. He stayed three days and three nights in the belly of a big fish.

7. He led the people into the promised land.

8. She gave fruit to her husband in the Garden of Eden.

9. She hid two spies in Jericho.

10. He washed his hands in a bowl of water.

Answers to
be found
on page 18

Bible who's who?

1. Who was a helper of Paul?
    a. Stephen **b.** Silas **c.** James **d.** Matthias

2. Who was a judge of Israel?
    a. Jehu **b.** Josiah **c.** Jepthah **d.** Uzziah

3. Who did Paul have a serious disagreement with?
    a. Luke **b.** Timothy **c.** Lydia **d.** Barnabas

4. Who was the first king of Israel?
    a. David **b.** Solomon **c.** Saul **d.** Rehoboam

5. Which helper of Paul deserted him half-way through a tour?
    a. John Mark **b.** Silas **c.** Timothy **d.** Demas

6. Who was a runaway slave but became like a son to Paul?
    a. Philemon **b.** Epaphras **c.** Onesimus **d.** Demas

7. Who was a prophet of Israel?
    a. Hezekiah **b.** Hoshea **c.** Sennacherrib **d.** Ezekiel

8. Who wrote to tell the people to rebuild the Temple?
    a. Haggai **b.** Jeremiah **c.** Joel **d.** Jonah

9. According to Mark, who did not take spices to Jesus' tomb?
    a. Mary Magdalene
    b. Salome
    c. Martha
    d. Mary the mother of James

10. Who was a rabbi?
    a. Gamaliel **b.** Gedaliah
    c. Amos **d.** Goliath

Answers to be found on page 18

Kings and queens

1. Which king was very wise?

2. Which future king killed Goliath?

3. Which king said he wanted to visit baby Jesus?

4. Which king built the first Temple?

5. Which king tried to kill David?

6. Which Jewish girl became queen of Persia?

7. Which queen came to visit Solomon?

8. Which king was married to Jezebel?

9. Which king beheaded John the Baptist?

10. What was the name of the king the wise men brought gifts to?

Answers to be found on page 18

Bible women

1. Who was the queen of Ethiopia when Philip met an Ethiopian official?
    a. Elizabeth **b.** Candace **c.** Esther **d.** Jezebel

2. Which relative of Jesus stood at the cross with Mary?
    a. Joseph **b.** His grandmother **c.** His aunt **d.** His uncle

3. Ruth was...
    a. an Israelite **b.** a Hittite **c.** a Roman **d.** a Moabite

4. Who listened to Paul when he was a prisoner in Caesarea, along with her brother, King Agrippa?
    a. Belulah **b.** Bernice **c.** Beatrice **d.** Bertha

5. Who was the wife of Felix, the Roman governor who kept Paul in prison for two years?
    a. Drusilla **b.** Potiphera **c.** Barbara **d.** Tryphosa

6. Who did Paul beg not to argue with Euodia?
    a. Priscilla **b.** Syntyche **c.** Lydia **d.** Beatrice

7. Who was Ruth's sister-in-law?
    a. Naomi **b.** Orpah **c.** Abishag **d.** Esther

8. Who gave David and his men a supply of food?
    a. Miriam **b.** Rahab **c.** Abigail **d.** Sarah

9. What was Ruth's relationship to King David?
    a. Granddaughter **b.** Great-grandmother
    c. Aunt **d.** Sister

10. Who said to Mary, the mother of Jesus, "Blessed are you among women... "?
    a. Elizabeth **b.** Herodias
    c. Diana **d.** Martha

Answers to be found on page 18

Odd one out

1. Who was not an apostle?
   a. Peter b. Stephen
   c. Matthew d. Nathanael

2. Which is not an Old Testament character?
   a. Rebekah b. Sarah
   c. Jessica d. Rachel

3. Who was not a "father of Israel"?
   a. Isaac b. Ishmael
   c. Abraham d. Jacob

4. Who is the odd one out?
   a. Mark b. Matthew c. Peter d. John

5. Who was not a child of Adam and Eve?
   a. Abel b. Cain c. Jeremy d. Seth

6. Which of these were not thrown into a fiery furnace?
   a. Shadrach b. Meshach
   c. Abednego d. Daniel

7. Which prophet does not have a book in the Bible?
   a. Isaiah b. Ezekiel c. Elijah d. Amos

8. Who was not a son of Noah?
   a. Japeth b. Shem c. Bacon d. Ham

9. Who is the odd one out?
   a. James d. Paul c. John d. Jude

10. Who is not mentioned in the Book of Judges?
    a. Gideon b. Samson
    c. Deborah d. Samuel

Answers to be found on page 18

Orders

1. Who was told to build a great ark?

2. Who was told to go to Nineveh?

3. Who were told to leave the Garden of Eden?

4. Who was told to march around Jericho?

5. Who was told to leave his father's house in Haran?

6. Who was told to leave Sodom?

7. Who was told to bathe in the River Jordan?

8. Who was told to come out of his tomb?

9. Who was told he must be born again?

10. Who was told to come down from a sycamore-fig tree?

Answers to
be found
on page 18

Names and name changes

1. What was Abraham's original name?
   a. Ari b. Abner c. Abram d. Abbie

2. What was Sarah's original name?
   a. Sardis b. Sarai c. Sally d. Seraphim

3. Who was told to give names to all the animals?
   a. Adam b. David c. Daniel d. Eve

4. What was Peter's original name?
   a. Simon b. Petrus c. Pete d. Simeon

5. What was Paul's original name?
   a. Sargon b. Salmon
   c. Salman d. Saul

6. What baby's name means "drew him out of the water"?
   a. David b. Moses c. Peter d. Paul

7. Who told Mary to call her baby "Jesus"?
   a. No one b. Joseph
   c. The angel Gabriel d. Her dad

8. Who was known as "The second (or last) Adam"?
   a. Cain b. Jesus
   c. John the Baptist d. Eve

9. Who called himself "The voice of one crying in the wilderness"?
   a. Elijah b. John the Baptist
   c. Jesus d. Moses

10. Jesus' name for himself was the "Son of Man".
    True or false?

Answers to be found on page 19

Prophets and judges

1. Which prophet hid by the brook
    Kerith (Cherith)?
    a. Elisha b. Eli c. Elymas d. Elijah

2. Who was the only woman judge to
    rule over Israel?
    a. Miriam b. Rebekah
    c. Deborah d. Hannah

3. Which prophet lay on his left side
    for 390 days as a sign of Jerusalem's
    destruction?
    a. Jeremiah b. Obadiah
    c. Habakkuk d. Ezekiel

4. Which prophet was called a traitor
    for preaching non-resistance?
    a. Hosea b. Jeremiah
    c. Malachi d. Micah

5. Who condemned a king with a
    parable about a lamb?
    a. Nathan b. Naboth
    c. Naaman d. Nahum

6. Who said, "I will moan like an owl"?
    a. Jeremiah b. Hosea
    c. Micah d. David

7. To which fearful man did an angel
    say, "The Lord is with you, mighty
    warrior"?
    a. Jeremiah b. Barak
    c. Sisera d. Gideon

8. Which prophetess forecast disaster
    when Josiah found the book of
    the law?
    a. Jedidiah b. Adaiah
    c. Huldah d. Hilkiah

9. Which left-handed judge killed
    a king with a sword hidden on
    his right leg?
    a. Ehud b. Eglon c. Sisera d. Othniel

10. Which prophet had all his writings cut
    up and burnt by a king?
    a. Hosea b. Jeremiah
    c. Micah d. Amos

Answers to be found on page 19

Kings

1. Who was king of Israel when Elijah was a prophet?
   a. Asa b. Ahab c. David d. Solomon

2. Which king put Daniel in the lions' den?
   a. Nebuchadnezzar b. Herod
   c. Belshazzar d. Darius

3. Which king stole a vineyard from Naboth?
   a. David b. Solomon
   c. Rehoboam d. Ahab

4. Who was not a king of Judah?
   a. Ahaziah b. Uzziah c. Omri d. Amon

5. To which king did Abraham say, "I will accept nothing from you, not even a thread"?
   a. King of Salem b. King of Shinar
   c. King of Elam d. King of Sodom

6. Who was the king of Judah when the Babylonians destroyed Jerusalem?
   a. Zedekiah b. Jehoiakim
   c. Jehoiachin d. Herod

7. What did King Hiram of Tyre give David when David became king?
   a. His daughter's hand in marriage
   b. Chariots and horses
   c. He built a palace d. Gold

8. Which son of Herod the Great became king of Judea on Herod's death?
   a. Archelaus b. Herod Philip
   c. Antipater d. Agrippa

9. Which king destroyed Jerusalem and deported its inhabitants?
   a. Vlad b. Nebuchadnezzar
   c. Evil-Merodach d. Belshazzar

10. Which king told the Jews they were free from exile in Babylon?
    a. Antaxerxes b. Cyrus
    c. Xerxes d. Darius

Answers to be found on page 19

Prophets and prophecies

1. Which prophet was put in a mucky pit?

2. Which prophet left his cloak for his successor?

3. Which prophet ran away to sea?

4. Who fed 100 men with twenty small loaves?

5. Which prophet had a talking donkey?

6. Which prophet explained Nebuchadnezzar's dream of a gigantic statue?

7. Which prophet talked with Jesus and Moses?

8. Which prophet wrote that the Messiah would be born of a virgin?

9. The coming of the Holy Spirit on the Day of Pentecost fulfilled the words of which prophet?

10. Why was Daniel put into the lions' den?

Answers to be found on page 19

Jesus' friends

1. According to Matthew, who did Jesus call as they were mending their nets?

2. Which tax collector did Jesus call?

3. According to John, who did Jesus call after he had seen him sitting under a fig tree?

4. Who poured perfume on Jesus' feet?

5. Who did Jesus ask to baptize him?

6. Who was the brother of Mary and Martha?

7. Which little man climbed a tree to get a good view of Jesus?

8. Who was the blind beggar who followed Jesus after Jesus restored his sight?

9. To whom did Jesus say, "Get behind me, Satan!"?

10. Who thought Jesus was a gardener?

Answers to be found on page 19

The twelve disciples

1. What city was Andrew from?
   a. Bethany b. Capernaum
   c. Bethsaida d. Jerusalem

2. Before he was a disciple, Matthew was a...
   a. Pharisee b. Soldier
   c. Fisherman d. Tax collector

3. To which disciple did some Greeks say, "Sir, we would like to see Jesus"?
   a. Andrew b. Philip
   c. Judas d. Nathanael

4. Who said, "My Lord and my God!" when he knew Jesus had risen from the dead?
   a. Peter b. John c. Mark d. Thomas

5. Which disciple told Jesus about the boy with the five loaves and two fish?
   a. Philip b. Andrew
   c. Matthew d. Peter

6. Which of these disciples of Jesus was first a disciple of John the Baptist?
   a. Nathanael b. Judas
   c. James d. Andrew

7. Which of Peter's relatives did Jesus heal of a fever?
   a. Wife b. Brother's wife
   c. Mother-in-law d. Nephew

8. Which disciple did not want Jesus to wash his feet?
   a. John b. James c. Andrew d. Peter

9. Which disciple was called the Zealot?
   a. Philip b. Simon c. Thomas d. Judas

10. What was Andrew doing when Jesus called him to be a disciple?
    a. Collecting taxes
    b. Fishing c. Reading
    d. Listening to John the Baptist

Answers to be found on page 19

Name the character

1. Samuel (1 Samuel 16:1–13)
2. Ruth (Ruth 1:15–18)
3. Lot's wife (Genesis 19:26)
4. David (1 Samuel 16:14–23)
5. Stephen (Acts 7:54–60)
6. Jonah (Jonah 1:17)
7. Joshua (Joshua 1:1–2)
8. Eve (Genesis 3:6)
9. Rahab (Joshua 2:4)
10. Pilate (Matthew 27:24)

Bible's who's who?

1. Silas (Acts 15:40)
2. Jepthah (Judges 12:7)
3. Barnabas (Acts 15:39)
4. Saul (1 Samuel 10:20–25)
5. John Mark (Acts 13:13; 15:37–38)
6. Onesimus (Philemon 9–10)
7. Ezekiel (Ezekiel 1:3)
8. Haggai (Haggai 1:3–4)
9. Martha (Mark 16:1)
10. Gamaliel (Acts 5:34)

Kings and queens

1. Solomon (1 Kings 4:30)
2. David (1 Samuel 17)
3. Herod the Great (Matthew 2:8)
4. Solomon (1 Kings 6:2)
5. Saul (1 Samuel 19:1)
6. Esther (Esther 2:17)
7. The Queen of Sheba (1 Kings 6:2)
8. Ahab (1 Kings 16:31)
9. Herod Antipas (Matthew 14:1–10)
10. Jesus

Bible women

1. Candace (Acts 8:26–39)
2. His aunt (John 19:25)
3. Moabite (Ruth 1:4)
4. Bernice (Acts 25:13–26)
5. Drusilla (Acts 24:24)
6. Syntyche (Philippians 4:2)
7. Orpah (Ruth 1:4)
8. Abigail (1 Samuel 25:18–20)
9. Great-grandmother (Ruth 4:17)
10. Elizabeth (Luke 1:41–42)

Odd one out

1. Stephen
2. Jessica
3. Ishmael
4. Peter (the others are Gospel writers)
5. Jeremy
6. Daniel
7. Elijah
8. Bacon
9. Paul (no letter is named after him)
10. Samuel

Orders

1. Noah (Genesis 6:13–14)
2. Jonah (Jonah 1:1–2)
3. Adam and Eve (Genesis 3:23)
4. Joshua (Joshua 6:2–3)
5. Abram (Abraham) (Genesis 11:31 – 12:3)
6. Lot (Genesis 19:1, 12–15)
7. Naaman (2 Kings 5:9–10)
8. Lazarus (John 11:43)
9. Nicodemus (John 3:1, 7)
10. Zacchaeus (Luke 19:5)

Names and name changes

1. Abram (Genesis 17:5)
2. Sarai (Genesis 17:15)
3. Adam (Genesis 2:19)
4. Simon (John 1:42)
5. Saul (Acts 13:9)
6. Moses (Exodus 2:10)
7. The angel Gabriel (Luke 1:31)
8. Jesus (1 Corinthians 15:45–48)
9. John the Baptist (Matthew 3:1–3)
10. True (e.g. Luke 19:10)

Prophets and Judges

1. Elijah (I Kings 17:3)
2. Deborah (Judges 4:4)
3. Ezekiel (Ezekiel 4:1–5)
4. Jeremiah (Jeremiah 38:1–4)
5. Nathan (2 Samuel 12:1–15)
6. Micah (Micah 1:8)
7. Gideon (Judges 6:12)
8. Huldah (2 Kings 22:14–18)
9. Ehud (Judges 3:20–23)
10. Jeremiah (Jeremiah 36:22–23)

Kings

1. Ahab (1 Kings 17:1)
2. Darius (Daniel 6)
3. Ahab (1 Kings 21:1–16)
4. Omri (1 Kings 16:23)
5. King of Sodom (Genesis 14:22–23)
6. Zedekiah (Jeremiah 39:1–3)
7. He built a palace (2 Samuel 5:11)
8. Archelaus (Matthew 2:22)
9. Nebuchadnezzar (Jeremiah 52:12–14)
10. Cyrus (Ezra 1)

Prophets and prophecies

1. Jeremiah (Jeremiah 38:6)
2. Elijah (2 Kings 2:13)
3. Jonah (Jonah 1:3)
4. Elisha (2 Kings 4:42–44)
5. Balaam (Numbers 22:28–30)
6. Daniel (Daniel 2:24–45)
7. Elijah (Mark 9:4–8)
8. Isaiah (Isaiah 7:14)
9. Joel (Acts 2:16–21)
10. For praying to God (Daniel 6:10–13)

Jesus' friends

1. James and John (Matthew 4:21)
2. Matthew (Levi) (Matthew 9:9)
3. Nathanael (John 1:43–50)
4. Mary, the sister of Martha (John 12:3)
5. John the Baptist (Matthew 3:13–15)
6. Lazarus (John 11:1–2)
7. Zacchaeus (Luke 19:1–10)
8. Bartimaeus (Mark 10:46–52)
9. Peter (Mark 8:33)
10. Mary Magdalene (John 20:15)

The twelve disciples

1. Capernaum (Mark 1:21, 29)
2. Tax collector (Matthew 9:9)
3. Philip (John 12:21)
4. Thomas (John 20:28)
5. Andrew (John 6:8–9)
6. Andrew (John 1:40)
7. Mother-in-law (Mark 1:29–31)
8. Peter (John 13:8)
9. Simon (Luke 6:15)
10. Fishing (Matthew 4:18–20)

Bible pairs

Complete the following pairs:

1. Adam and...

2. Peter and...

3. James and...

4. David and...

5. Elijah and...

6. Ahab and...

7. Samson and...

8. Aquila and...

9. Jacob and...

10. Cain and...

Answers to be found on page 30

Husbands and wives

1. Who was the wicked wife of King Ahab?

2. What was the name of Abraham's wife?

3. Who was Michal's husband?

4. Whose wife told him not to harm Jesus?

5. What were the names of Jacob's two wives?

6. Who was Rebekah's husband?

7. Who was Aquila married to?

8. Who was Moses's wife?

9. Who was Ananias married to?

10. Who did Ruth marry?

Answers to be found on page 30

Fathers and sons

1. Who set out to sacrifice his son, Isaac?

2. Who was the father of Jonathan?

3. Who was the father of Cain, Abel, and Seth?

4. Who was the father of Joseph and his brothers?

5. Which king was David's son?

6. Who was Jacob's father?

7. Who was the father of Shem, Ham, and Japheth?

8. Who was father of James and John?

9. Who was Esau's father?

10. According to the Bible, who is the father of the Jews and all people of faith?

Answers to
be found on
page 30

Brothers and sisters

1. Who were Abel's brothers?

2. Who was Moses's brother?

3. Who was Joseph's younger brother?

4. Who were Ham's brothers?

5. Who was Simon Peter's brother?

6. Which brothers were called the "Sons of Thunder"?

7. Who was Leah's sister?

8. Who did Jesus say are his brothers and sisters?

9. What was the name of Isaac's half-brother?

10. Who was Jacob's twin brother?

Answers to be found on page 30

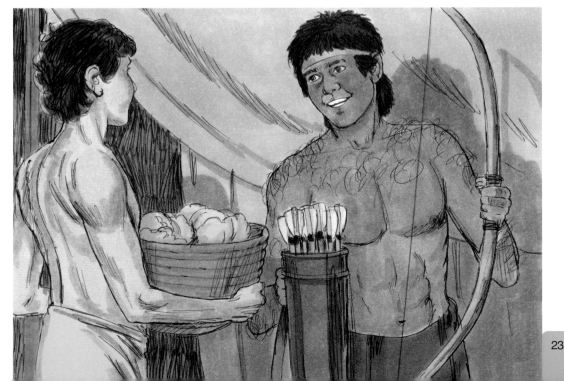

Sons and daughters

1. Which mother brought her son, Samuel, a coat every year?
   a. Hagar b. Hannah c. Haggai d. Anna

2. Whose daughter died while Jesus was on his way to his house to heal her?
   a. Jairus b. James c. Jonah d. Jacob

3. How many sons did Jacob have?
   a. 10 b. 12 c. 14 d. 15

4. What did the Shunammite's son do when Elisha brought him back to life?
   a. Coughed b. Sneezed seven times c. Yawned d. Laughed

5. To whose mother did an angel say he would grow up to be "a wild donkey of a man"?
   a. Esau b. Samson c. Ishmael d. Saul

6. Manasseh was one of Joseph's sons. Who was the other?
   a. Simeon b. Zebulun c. Issachar d. Ephraim

7. Where was Jesus when he brought back to life the only son of a widow?
   a. Capernaum b. Bethany c. Jericho d. Nain

8. Who does Paul write to and call, "My true son in the faith"?
   a. Titus b. Silas c. Luke d. Timothy

9. Who called her son a name meaning "he laughs"?
   a. Hagar b. Sarah c. Rebekah d. Rachel

10. How old was Abraham when his son Isaac was born?
    a. 50 b. 100 c. 60 d. 110

Answers to be found on page 30

Bible children

1. Who heard God calling his name and thought the priest was calling him?

2. What was the name of the first baby to be born?

3. What did a boy offer Jesus to feed 5,000 people?

4. What did Jesus tell Jairus to do when his daughter was brought back to life?

5. Where did Mary and Joseph find Jesus when they lost him in Jerusalem?

6. Where was Moses brought up as a child?

7. Which baby boy was born six months before Jesus?

8. What did the disciples do when mothers brought their children to Jesus?

9. Which twin was the firstborn and the one his father Isaac loved the most?

10. Which boy dreamed his brothers' sheaves of corn were bowing down to his?

Answers to be found on page 30

Bible babes

1. Which widow met the baby Jesus at the Temple?
   a. Anna b. Mary Magdalene
   c. Lydia d. Priscilla

2. Who became king when he was seven and repaired the Temple?
   a. Jehu b. Joash c. Josiah d. David

3. Whose mother laid him in a basket among the reeds?
   a. Daniel b. Moses
   c. Joshua d. Samson

4. Which toddler was dropped by his nurse and crippled?
   a. Josiah b. Evil-Merodach
   c. Mephibosheth d. Ish-Bosheth

5. Which baby had a Christian mother and grandmother?
   a. Timothy b. Titus c. Silas d. Luke

6. Which baby's birth was announced by an angel who went up to heaven in a flame?
   a. Samuel b. Samson
   c. Isaac d. Gideon

7. Who was Boaz's son?
   a. Obed b. David c. Jesse d. Solomon

8. Whose mother prayed so hard for a son that the priest thought she was drunk?
   a. Samuel b. Samson
   c. Saul d. Gideon

9. What baby was left under a shrub in Beersheba to die?
   a. Isaac b. Ishmael
   c. Jacob d. Solomon

10. To whom did God say, "Before you were born I set you apart... "?
    a. Paul b. Timothy
    c. Jeremiah d. Abraham

Answers to be found on page 31

Bible fathers

1. Who was the father of Absalom?
   a. Rehoboam b. Saul c. David d. Solomon

2. Who was the father of Alexander and Rufus?
   a. Nicodemus b. Simon of Cyrene c. Philemon d. Barnabas

3. Who was the father of Mephibosheth?
   a. Jonathan b. David c. Jacob b. Joseph

4. Who was the father of Michal?
   a. David b. Saul c. Jacob d. Moses

5. Who was the father of Manasseh and Ephraim?
   a. Reuben b. Simeon c. Levi d. Joseph

6. Who was the father-in-law of Caiaphas?
   a. Annas b. Gamaliel c. Antipas d. Ananias

7. Who was the father of Dinah?
   a. David b. Jacob c. Solomon d. Ahab

8. Who was the father of Jonathan?
   a. Solomon b. Saul c. David d. Hezekiah

9. Who was Joshua's father?
   a. Moses b. Caleb c. Jeshurun d. Nun

10. Who was the father of James, leader of the Jerusalem church?
    a. Simeon b. Zechariah
    c. Joseph d. We don't know

Answers to be found on page 31

Love stories

1. Who had to work seven years for his wife but loved her so much they seemed like a few days?
   a. Isaac b. Jacob c. Joseph d. David

2. Who loved her mother-in-law so much that she left her own country to go with her?
   a. Rachel b. Rebekah
   c. Ruth d. Rahab

3. Which arranged marriage became a love marriage, so the husband was comforted after his mother's death?
   a. Sarah and Abraham
   b. Rebekah and Isaac
   c. Rachel and Jacob
   d. Ruth and Boaz

4. Which prophet had an unfaithful wife, but loved her and forgave her?
   a. Ezekiel b. Daniel c. Hosea d. Joel

5. Whose love for a Philistine woman destroyed his strength?
   a. Barak b. Gideon c. Samson d. David

6. Who wrote, "Your love for me was wonderful, more wonderful than that of women"?
   a. Abraham b. Moses
   c. David d. Solomon

7. To which childless wife did her husband say, "Don't I mean more to you than ten sons"?
   a. Sarah b. Rachel
   c. Hannah d. Elizabeth

8. In which book of the Bible does the loved one say, "His banner over me be love"?
   a. Psalms b. Song of Solomon
   c. Ecclesiastes d. Lamentations

9. In which book do we read, "Whoever does not love does not know God, because God is love"?
   a. 1 Thessalonians b. 1 Corinthians
   c. 1 Peter d. 1 John

10. Who wrote, "If I have not love I am a clanging cymbal"?
    a. Paul b. Peter c. John d. James

Answers to be found on page 31

Successors

1. Which prophet succeeded Elijah?

2. Which leader of Israel succeeded Moses?

3. Which companion of Paul took the place of Barnabas?

4. Which apostle succeeded Judas Iscariot?

5. Which king succeeded Saul?

6. Which patriarch succeeded Abraham?

7. Which king succeeded the prophet Samuel?

8. Which disciple looked after Mary, the mother of Jesus, after Jesus died and rose again?

9. Which judge of Israel succeeded Eli?

10. Which king succeeded Solomon?

Answers to be found on page 31

Bible pairs

1. Eve
2. Andrew
3. John
4. Jonathan (or Goliath)
5. Elisha
6. Jezebel
7. Delilah
8. Priscilla
9. Esau
10. Abel

Husbands and wives

1. Jezebel (1 Kings 21:4–5)
2. Sarah (Genesis 17:15)
3. King David (1 Samuel 19:11)
4. Pontius Pilate (Matthew 27:17–19)
5. Leah and Rachel (Genesis 29:16–28)
6. Isaac (Genesis 24:67)
7. Priscilla (Acts 18:2)
8. Zipporah (Exodus 2:21)
9. Sapphira (Acts 5:1)
10. Boaz (Ruth 4:13)

Fathers and sons

1. Abraham (Genesis 22:1–2)
2. Saul (1 Samuel 14:49)
3. Adam (Genesis 4:1–2, 25)
4. Jacob (Genesis 35:23–26)
5. Solomon (1 Kings 2:1)
6. Isaac (Genesis 25:21–26)
7. Noah (Genesis 5:32)
8. Zebedee (Matthew 4:21)
9. Isaac (Genesis 25, 23–26)
10. Abraham (Galatians 3:7)

Brothers and sisters

1. Cain and Seth (Genesis 4:1, 25)
2. Aaron (Exodus 4:14)
3. Benjamin (Genesis 46:19)
4. Shem and Japheth (Genesis 9:18)
5. Andrew (John 1:40)
6. James and John (Mark 3:17)
7. Rachel (Genesis 29:16)
8. Those who do his will (Matthew 12:50)
9. Ishmael (Genesis 25:9, 12)
10. Esau (Genesis 25:25–26)

Sons and daughters

1. Hannah (1 Samuel 2:19)
2. Jairus (Mark 5:22–43)
3. 12 (Genesis 35:22–26)
4. Sneezed seven times (2 Kings 4:35)
5. Ishmael (Genesis 16:7–12)
6. Ephraim (Genesis 41:50–52)
7. Nain (Luke 7:11–16)
8. Timothy (1 Timothy 1:2)
9. Sarah (Genesis 21:1–7)
10. 100 (Genesis 21:5)

Bible children

1. Samuel (1 Samuel 3:3–8)
2. Cain (Genesis 4:1)
3. Five loaves and two fish (John 6:9)
4. He told them to give her something to eat (Mark 5:43)
5. In the Temple (Luke 2:46)
6. In Pharaoh's palace (Exodus 2:10)
7. John the Baptist (Luke 1:26, 36)
8. They told them to go away (Mark 10:13)
9. Esau (Genesis 25:25, 28)
10. Joseph (Genesis 37:7)

Bible babes

1. Anna (Luke 2:36–38)
2. Joash (2 Kings 11:21; 12:1–14)
3. Moses (Exodus 2:3)
4. Mephibosheth (2 Samuel 4:4)
5. Timothy (2 Timothy 1:5)
6. Samson (Judges 13:3, 20, 24)
7. Obed (Ruth 4:21)
8. Samuel (1 Samuel 1:12–20)
9. Ishmael (Genesis 16:15; 21:14–21)
10. Jeremiah (Jeremiah 1:5)

Bible fathers

1. David (2 Samuel 13:37)
2. Simon of Cyrene (Mark 15:21)
3. Jonathan (2 Samuel 4:4)
4. Saul (1 Samuel 18:20)
5. Joseph (Genesis 48:1)
6. Annas (John 18:13)
7. Jacob (Genesis 34:1)
8. Saul (2 Samuel 9:6)
9. Nun (Joshua 1:1)
10. Joseph (Galatians 1:19)

Love stories

1. Jacob (Genesis 29:20)
2. Ruth (Ruth 1:16)
3. Rebekah and Isaac (Genesis 24:67)
4. Hosea (Hosea 3:1)
5. Samson (Judges 16:1–21)
6. David (2 Samuel 1:26)
7. Hannah (1 Samuel 1:8)
8. Song of Solomon (2:4)
9. 1 John (4:8))
10. Paul (1 Corinthians 13:1)

Successors

1. Elisha (2 Kings 2:15)
2. Joshua (Joshua 1:1–2)
3. Silas (Acts 15:39–40)
4. Matthias (Acts 1:26)
5. David (1 Samuel 16:1, 13)
6. Isaac (Genesis 25:11)
7. Saul (1 Samuel 8:22; 10:1)
8. John (John 19:26–27)
9. Samuel (1 Samuel 3; 7:15)
10. Rehoboam (1 Kings 11:43)

Bible mountains

On which mount or mountain...:

1. ... did Moses receive the Ten Commandments?

2. ... did the Ark land?

3. ... did Deborah's chariots beat the Philistines?

4. ... did Moses die?

5. ... was the Garden of Gethsemane?

6. ... did Elijah challenge the prophets of Baal?

7. ... did an angel tell Abraham not to kill Isaac?

8. ... was Saul killed in battle?

9. ... was the Temple situated?

10. ... did Jesus ascend to heaven?

Answers to be found on page 38

Hometowns

1. Who said, of Jesus' hometown, "Can anything good come from there?"
   a. Caiaphas b. Herod
   c. Nathanael d. Pontius Pilate

2. Where was Paul's birthplace?
   a. Damascus b. Jerusalem
   c. Athens d. Tarsus

3. Where did Abraham come from originally?
   a. Ur b. Haran c. Sidon d. Gomorrah

4. Where did Peter live?
   a. Nazareth b. Capernaum
   c. Bethany d. Bethlehem

5. Which island did Barnabas come from?
   a. Malta b. Crete c. Cyprus d. Sicily

6. Where did Ruth's mother-in-law come from?
   a. Nazareth b. Jerusalem
   c. Capernaum d. Bethlehem

7. Where did Timothy live?
   a. Corinth b. Lystra
   c. Ephesus d. Tyre

8. Where did Zacchaeus the tax collector come from?
   a. Jericho b. Jerusalem
   c. Capernaum d. Cana

9. Where did Amos the prophet come from?
   a. Moresheth b. Tekoa
   c. Elkosh d. Jerusalem

10. Where was the palace of King Ahab?
    a. Bethel b. Samaria
    c. Jerusalem d. Jericho

Answers to be found on page 38

Jerusalem

1. Who lived in Jerusalem before the Israelites?
   a. Rechabites b. Moabites
   c. Philistines d. Jebusites

2. Who died because he touched the Ark as David was bringing it to Jerusalem?
   a. Uzzah b. Noah
   c. Paul d. Obed-Edom

3. Who said, "O Jerusalem, Jerusalem, you who kill the prophets… "?
   a. Jeremiah b. Micah
   c. Jesus d. John the Baptist

4. A king of Jerusalem brought bread and wine to Abram (Abraham). What was his name?
   a. David b. Melchizedek
   c. Zedekiah d. Solomon

5. Who rebuilt the wall of Jerusalem after the exile?
   a. Ezra b. Nehemiah
   c. Solomon d. Zerubbabel

6. God told Jeremiah he would break Jerusalem like a… ?
   a. Potter's jar b. Bruised reed
   c. Egg d. Window

7. When there was a riot in Jerusalem, who rescued Paul?
   a. An angel
   b. The Roman commander
   c. Pilate d. Gamaliel

8. Whose mother had a house in Jerusalem where the early church met?
   a. Peter b. Matthew
   c. John Mark d. Thomas

9. Which king ran away from Jerusalem at night with his entire army, through the gate by his garden?
   a. Zedekiah b. Jehoiachin
   c. David d. Rehoboam

10. Who captured Jerusalem by going through a water tunnel?
    a. Hezekiah b. Nebuchadnezzar
    c. Joshua d. David

Answers to be found on page 38

Landmarks

1. Which river is not in the Bible?
   a. Jordan b. Nile
   c. Pharpar d. Amazon

2. Which mountain is not in the Bible?
   a. Ararat b. Everest
   c. Sinai d. Hermon

3. Which island is not in the Bible?
   a. Crete b. Rhodes c. Sicily d. Samos

4. Which garden is not in the Bible?
   a. Eden b. Gethsemane
   c. Versailles d. Paradise

5. Where did the Israelites first set up camp after crossing the Red Sea?
   a. Sinai b. Jericho
   c. Elim d. Damascus

6. Where did Gideon and the Israelites beat the Midianites?
   a. Below the hill of Moreh
   b. Valley of Elah c. Hazor d. Gaza

7. Where did Jacob build an altar after fleeing his brother, Esau?
   a. Shechem b. Hebron
   c. Elbethel d. Samaria

8. Which lake did Jesus and his disciples sail across?
   a. Lake Hula b. Red Sea
   c. Dead Sea d. Sea of Galilee

9. Where was Jesus baptized?
   a. Jordan River b. Yarmuk River
   c. Jabbok River d. Arnon River

10. Where did God confuse the language as the people built a tower?
    a. Babylon b. Beersheba
    c. Babel d. Bethel

Answers to be found on page 38

Towns and villages

1. Where did Elijah raise the widow's son?
   a. Bethel b. Zarephath
   c. Bethlehem d. Shiloh

2. Where did Jonah board a ship to Tarshish?
   a. Joppa b. Tyre c. Ashdod d. Gaza

3. Where did Jesus' family live?
   a. Capernaum b. Jericho
   c. Ephraim d. Nazareth

4. Where did Jesus meet a Samaritan woman at a well?
   a. Tiberias b. Lydda
   c. Sychar d. Bethlehem

5. Where was the wedding where Jesus turned water into wine?
   a. Nazareth b. Cana
   c. Jerusalem d. Caesarea

6. Where did Jesus' friends Mary and Martha live?
   a. Bethany b. Bethel
   c. Hebron d. Beersheba

7. Which town was Jesus approaching when he met Bartimaeus?
   a. Jerusalem b. Jericho
   c. Caesarea d. Bethany

8. Which town was near to where Jesus fed more than 5,000 people?
   a. Lydda b. Cana
   c. Bethsaida d. Bethlehem

9. In which town was Saul baptized?
   a. Jerusalem b. Damascus
   c. Tyre d. Antioch

10. In which town did Peter meet Cornelius?
    a. Caesarea b. Jericho
    c. Alexandria d. Athens

Answers to be found on page 38

Journeys

1. Where was Joseph taken by the Midianite traders?
   a. Mesopotamia b. Egypt
   c. Syria d. Macedonia

2. To which place did Naomi take Ruth?
   a. Nazareth b. Jerusalem
   c. Cana d. Bethlehem

3. Where was the king's palace where Daniel and his friends were taken?
   a. Nineveh b. Babylon
   c. Ur d. Damascus

4. To which town was the Good Samaritan journeying?
   a. Jericho b. Jerusalem
   c. Bethlehem d. Samaria

5. Who "resolutely set out for Jerusalem"?
   a. David b. Jesus
   c. Paul d. Daniel

6. On the first Easter, to which village were Jesus' followers going when Jesus walked with them?
   a. Emmaus b. Jericho
   c. Bethany d. Nazareth

7. Where was Paul going when Jesus appeared to him?
   a. Emmaus b. Rome
   c. Damascus d. Ephesus

8. To which country was Paul journeying when he was shipwrecked?
   a. Italy b. Spain c. Africa d. Greece

9. On which island was Paul shipwrecked on his voyage?
   a. Malta b. Cyprus c. Crete d. Lesbos

10. Which place did Paul not visit?
    a. Rome b. Paris
    c. Jerusalem d. Athens

Answers to be found on page 39

Bible mountains

1. Sinai (Horeb) (Exodus 19:18–20:17)
2. Ararat (Genesis 8:4)
3. Tabor (Judges 4:6–7)
4. Nebo (Deuteronomy 34:1)
5. Mount of Olives (Luke 22:39; Mark 14:26, 32)
6. Carmel (1 Kings 18; 19)
7. Moriah (Genesis 22; 2–12)
8. Gilboa (2 Samuel 1:21)
9. Zion (Moriah) (2 Samuel 5:7; 2 Chronicles 3:1)
10. Mount of Olives (Acts 1:12)

Hometowns

1. Nathanael (John 1:46)
2. Tarsus (Acts 21:39)
3. Ur (Genesis 11:31)
4. Capernaum (Mark 1:21, 29)
5. Cyprus (Acts 4:36)
6. Bethlehem (Ruth 1:1)
7. Lystra (Acts 16:1)
8. Jericho (Luke 19:1–2)
9. Tekoa (Amos 1:1)
10. Samaria (1 Kings 16:29; 20:43)

Jerusalem

1. Jebusites (Joshua 15:63)
2. Uzzah (2 Samuel 6:6–7)
3. Jesus (Mathew 23:37)
4. Melchizedek (Genesis 14:18–19)
5. Nehemiah (Nehemiah 2:17–20)
6. Potter's jar (Jeremiah 19:11)
7. The Roman commander (Acts 21:30–32)
8. John Mark (Acts 12:12)
9. Zedekiah (Jeremiah 52:7–9)
10. David (2 Samuel 5:6–9)

Landmarks

1. Amazon
2. Everest
3. Sicily
4. Versailles
5. Elim (Exodus 15:22–27)
6. Below the hill of Moreh (Judges 7:1)
7. Elbethel (Genesis 35:7)
8. Sea of Galilee (Tiberias) (John 6:1)
9. Jordan River (Matthew 3:13)
10. Babel (Genesis 11:9)

Towns and villages

1. Zarephath (I Kings 17:8–24)
2. Joppa (Jonah 1:3)
3. Nazareth (Luke 2:39–40)
4. Sychar (John 4:5–7)
5. Cana (John 2:1)
6. Bethany (John 11:1)
7. Jericho (Luke 18:35; Mark 10:46)
8. Bethsaida (Luke 9:10–17)
9. Damascus (Acts 9:10)
10. Caesarea (Acts 10:24–25)

Journeys

1. Egypt (Genesis 37:36)
2. Bethlehem (Ruth 1:22)
3. Babylon (Daniel 1)
4. Jericho (Luke 10:30)
5. Jesus (Luke 9:51)
6. Emmaus (Luke 24:13–15)
7. Damascus (Acts 9:3–5)
8. Italy (Acts 27:1)
9. Malta (Acts 28:1)
10. Paris

Books of the Old Testament

1. What is the first book in the Bible?

2. Name a book called after a woman.

3. Name a book full of wise sayings.

4. Name a book beginning with "Z".

5. Which book is a hymn book?

6. What is the last book of the Old Testament?

7. Which book comes after Genesis?

8. Which book is mostly about building city walls?

9. Who is said to have written the book of Numbers?

10. What is the fifth book of the Old Testament?

Answers to be found on page 50

Bible verses

1. What are the opening words of the Bible?

2. Which verse begins "God so loved the world..."?

3. Where would you find the words "The Lord is my shepherd..."?

4. What are the first words of John's Gospel?

5. What did Jesus say just before he died?

6. Where are the words "Here I am! I stand at the door and knock"?

7. Which chapter of Matthew's Gospel contains the Beatitudes?

8. What is the shortest verse in the Bible?

9. Which book begins "The revelation of Jesus Christ..."?

10. Which psalm has the most verses?

Answers to be
found on page 50

Where do you find... ?

In which book of the Bible will you find the following:

1. The story of the exodus?

2. The birth of John the Baptist?

3. "Shout for joy to the Lord, all the earth."

4. The story of creation?

5. The story of the wise men?

6. The letters to the seven churches of Asia Minor?

7. "For God so loved the world that he gave his one and only Son..."?

8. The story of Daniel in the lions' den?

9. Paul's journeys?

10. The story of Samson?

Answers to be found on page 50

Books of the New Testament

1. Which book follows Acts?

2. How many letters were written by the apostle Peter?

3. What is the last book in the Bible?

4. Name the four Gospels.

5. Name four letters by Paul.

6. What is the shortest book in the New Testament?

7. What language was the New Testament written in?

8. Which book follows Ephesians?

9. As well as his Gospel, what other book did Luke write?

10. Which book comes before Revelation?

Answers to be found on page 50

Complete the verse

Complete the following verses:

1. The Lord is my... and my salvation.

2. For God so loved the... that he gave his one and only Son.

3. In the beginning was the...

4. For all have... and fall short of the glory of God.

5. My soul... the Lord.

6. I have come that they might have... and have it to the full.

7. For God loves a cheerful...

8. I can do all this through him who gives me...

9. My father's house has many...

10. I am the... ; you are the branches.

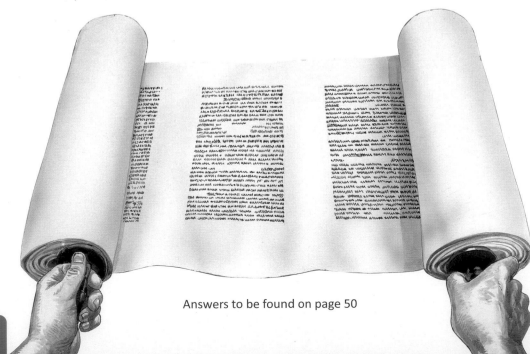

Answers to be found on page 50

Bible basics

1. How many books are in the Bible?
    a. 78 b. 66 d. 56 d. 32

2. In which book of the Bible do you find the Ten Commandments?
    a. Genesis b. Numbers c. Exodus d. Leviticus

3. Two books in the Bible are named after women. Which comes first?
    a. Esther b. Ruth

4. Who wrote the letter to Titus?
    a. Paul b. Mark c. Silas d. John

5. Which is the longest book in the Bible?
    a. Genesis b. Revelation c. Psalms d. Lamentations

6. Which is not an Old Testament book?
    a. Jeremiah b. Obadiah c. Hezekiah d. Zechariah

7. Which Gospels were not written by one of the twelve apostles?
    a. Matthew b. Mark c. Luke d. John

8. What is the eighth book in the Old Testament?
    a. Judges b. Joshua
    c. Ruth d. Leviticus

9. How many books are names of Old Testament prophets?
    a. 12 b. 14 c. 16 d. 18

10. How many books are in the New Testament?
    a. 26 b. 27 c. 28 d. 29

Answers to be found on page 50

Who said... ? part one

1. "Why wasn't this perfume sold and the money given to the poor?"
   a. Judas b. Simon c. Jesus d. Mary

2. "Let me die with the Philistines."
   a. Moses b. Elijah
   c. Samson d. Goliath

3. "What is truth?"
   a. Annas b. Pilate c. Jesus d. Peter

4. "Lord Jesus, receive my spirit."
   a. Paul b. John the Baptist
   c. Mary d. Stephen

5. "Am I my brother's keeper?"
   a. Jacob b. Joseph c. Cain d. Andrew

6. "Surely he was the Son of God!", when Jesus died on the cross.
   a. Pilate b. Roman centurion
   c. High priest d. Herod

7. "I know that my redeemer lives."
   a. Job b. David
   c. Mary Magdalene d. Paul

8. "The Lord is my shepherd."
   a. Peter b. Paul c. Mary d. David

9. "I am the good shepherd."
   a. Jesus b. David c. Peter d. Abraham

10. "Let us make mankind in our image."
    a. Peter b. Isaiah c. God d. Jeremiah

Answers to be found on page 51

Who said... ? part two

1. Who did Jesus ask, "Who do you say I am?"
   a. Mary b. Pontius Pilate
   c. Paul d. His disciples

2. Who did Jesus ask, "Do you betray me with a kiss?"
   a. Judas Iscariot b. Pontius Pilate
   c. Delilah d. Peter

3. Who did Jesus ask, "Why are you persecuting me?"
   a. Judas Iscariot b. King Herod
   c. Pontius Pilate d. Saul

4. Who said he was not worthy to undo Jesus' sandals?
   a. Paul b. Peter c. Stephen
   d. John the Baptist

5. Who told Moses to take off his sandals?
   a. Aaron b. Pharaoh
   c. An angel d. God

6. Who said, "It is better for you that one man die for the people than that the whole nation perish"?
   a. Jesus b. Paul
   c. Caiaphas d. Pilate

7. Of whom did Jesus say, "Theirs is the kingdom of heaven"?
   a. Children b. Angels
   c. Apostles d. The poor in spirit

8. Jesus' cry on the cross, "Eli, Eli, lema sabachthani", means:
   a. "Help me!" b. "My God, my God, why have you forsaken me?"
   c. "Elijah! Elijah!" d. "It is finished."

9. Jesus' words to Jairus's daughter, "Talitha koum!", means:
   a. "Little girl, get up!"
   b. "Hello, Tabitha!"
   c. We don't know

10. Who told Pilate, "Don't have anything to do with that innocent man"?
    a. Centurion b. His wife
    c. Chief priest d. Caesar

Answers to be found on page 51

Verse mix-up

Unscramble the verses:

1. Like sheep astray we all have gone

2. For the plans I know for you I have

3. The life and the resurrection I am

4. Fill you the God may all with peace of hope and joy

5. Of the house forever I will the Lord dwell in

6. All the trust in your Lord with heart

7. Like wings on eagles they soar will

8. Be anything not anxious about do

9. Everything a time there is for

10. A love you command one new I give another

Answers to be found on page 51

Bible knowledge

1. Which is not listed in 1 Corinthians 13?
   a. Faith b. Love c. Sympathy d. Hope

2. Who wrote, "Even though I walk through the darkest valley, I will fear no evil"?
   a. Paul b. We don't know c. David d. Jeremiah

3. Who wrote before a dangerous journey, "I was ashamed to ask the king for soldiers to protect us"?
   a. Abraham b. Ezra c. Nehemiah d. Zerubbabel

4. Who wrote, "If I have not love I am a clanging cymbal"?

5. In which book do we read, "Anyone who does not love remains in death"?

6. Of whom was it said, "He was more humble than anyone else on the face of the earth"?
   a. Jesus b. Moses c. Elijah d. Paul

7. Complete the verse: "These three remain: faith, hope and... but the greatest of these is...
   a. Joy b. Peace c. Love d. Patience

8. To whom did Jesus say, "No one can see the kingdom of God unless they are born again."
   a. Peter b. Andrew c. Nicodemus d. Caiaphas

9. Complete the verse: "So in everything... to others what you would have them... to you"

10. What are the words of the last verse of the Bible?

Answers to be found on page 51

Books of the Old Testament

1. Genesis
2. Ruth, Esther
3. Proverbs
4. Zechariah, Zephaniah
5. Psalms
6. Malachi
7. Exodus
8. Nehemiah
9. Moses
10. Deuteronomy

Bible verses

1. "In the beginning God…"
2. John 3:16
3. Psalm 23
4. "In the beginning was the Word…"
5. "It is finished." (John19:30)
6. Revelation 3:20
7. Chapter 5
8. "Jesus wept." (John 11:35)
9. Revelation
10. Psalm 119

Where do you find… ?

1. Exodus
2. Luke's Gospel
3. Psalms
4. Genesis
5. Matthew's Gospel
6. Revelation
7. John's Gospel
8. Daniel
9. Acts of the Apostles
10. Judges

Books of the New Testament

1. Romans
2. Two
3. Revelation
4. Matthew, Mark, Luke, John
5. Romans, Corinthians, Galatians, Ephesians, Philippians, Colossians, Thessalonians, Timothy, Titus, Philemon
6. 2 John
7. Greek
8. Philippians
9. Acts of the Apostles
10. Jude

Complete the verse

1. Light (Psalms 27:1)
2. World (John 3:16)
3. Word (John 1:1)
4. Sinned (Romans 3:23)
5. Glorifies (Luke 1:46)
6. Life (John 10:10)
7. Giver (2 Corinthians 9:7)
8. Strength (Philippians 4:13)
9. Rooms (John 14:2)
10. Vine (John 15:5)

Bible basics

1. 66
2. Exodus
3. Ruth
4. Paul
5. Psalms
6. Obadiah
7. Mark, Luke
8. Ruth
9. 16
10. 27

Who said… ? part one

1. Judas (John 12:4–6)
2. Samson (Judges 16:30)
3. Pilate (John 18:38)
4. Stephen (Acts 7:59)
5. Cain (Genesis 4:9)
6. Roman centurion (Matthew 27:54)
7. Job (Job 19:25)
8. David (Psalms 23:1)
9. Jesus (John 10:11)
10. God (Genesis 1:26)

Who said… ? part two

1. His disciples (Matthew 16: 13)
2. Judas Iscariot (Luke 22:48)
3. Saul (Acts 9:4)
4. John the Baptist (John 1:27)
5. God (Exodus 3:4–5)
6. Caiaphas (John 11:50)
7. The poor in spirit (Matthew 5:3)
8. "My God, my God, why have you forsaken me?" (Matthew 27:46)
9. "Little girl, get up!" (Mark 5:41)
10. His wife (Matthew 27:19)

Verse mix-up

1. We all, like sheep, have gone astray. (Isaiah 53:6)
2. For I know the plans I have for you. (Jeremiah 29:11)
3. I am the resurrection and the life. (John 11:25)
4. May the God of hope fill you with all joy and peace. (Romans 15:13)
5. I will dwell in the house of the Lord forever. (Psalms 23:6)
6. Trust in the Lord with all your heart. (Proverbs 3:5)
7. They will soar on wings like eagles. (Isaiah 40:31)
8. Do not be anxious about anything. (Philippians 4:6)
9. There is a time for everything. (Ecclesiastes 3:1)
10. A new command I give you: Love one another. (John 13:34)

Bible knowledge

1. Sympathy
2. David (Psalms 23:4)
3. Ezra (Ezra 8:22)
4. Paul (1 Corinthians 13:1)
5. 1 John (3:14)
6. Moses (Numbers 12:3)
7. Love (1 Corinthians 13:13)
8. Nicodemus (John 3:3)
9. Do (Matthew 7:12)
10. The grace of the Lord Jesus be with God's people. Amen

Sports and games

1. According to the letter to the Hebrews, what are we to do with perseverance?

2. In 1 Corinthians Paul said, "In a race all the runners run, but only one gets the..."

3. In Luke's gospel, what game were the children playing in Jesus' illustration of people who rejected both him and John?

4. In 1 Corinthians, what sport is Paul referring to when he says, "I don't beat the air"?

5. Who in the book of Judges thought up a riddle for a party?

6. What gaming equipment did soldiers most probably have at the foot of the cross?

7. In the Old Testament, what sport did Jonathan pretend to be playing when he sent a coded message to David?

8. What commandment prevented Jewish children playing with dolls?

9. Wrestling matches were popular, but who wrestled with an angel in the book of Genesis?

10. Who asked questions in an Old Testament quiz with camel-loads of prizes?

Answers to be found on page 60

Food, glorious food!

1. Who found honey inside the body of a dead lion?
   a. Jonah b. Samson c. David d. Ruth

2. Elisha purified a pot of stew that had been poisoned with...
   a. Lead b. Wild gourds
   c. Arsenic d. Bad cheese

3. What sort of bread did the Israelites eat at Passover?
   a. Sliced b. Wholemeal
   c. Unleavened d. Pitta

4. Who traded his birthright to his brother for lentil stew?
   a. Benjamin b. Peter c. Jacob d. Esau

5. What did John the Baptist eat in the wilderness?
   a. Lobsters b. Rabbits
   c. Quails d. Locusts

6. What did the widow make for the prophet Elijah?
   a. Beer b. Bread c. Stew d. Ice-cream

7. When Jesus made breakfast on the beach, what did the disciples eat?
   a. Bread and honey
   b. Bread and olives c. Bread and fish
   d. Bread and scrambled eggs

8. What did the people call the sweet flakes of food that God gave them to eat in the desert?
   a. Manna b. Halva
   c. Coriander d. Pitta

9. What did the spies sent by Moses not return with?
   a. Grapes b. Honey
   c. Pomegranates d. Figs

10. What tree did Jesus curse when it had no fruit on it?
    a. Fig b. Date c. Coconut d. Orange

Answers to be found on page 60

Buying, selling, and bribing

1. Who lied about how much he had got from the sale of some property?
   a. Judas b. Ananias
   c. Aquila d. Aeneas

2. Who condemned the people "for cheating with dishonest scales"?
   a. Micah b. Amos c. Isaiah
   d. John the Baptist

3. Who offered money in return for the power of the Holy Spirit?
   a. Demas b. Simon the sorcerer
   c. Bar-Jesus d. Tychicus

4. Who gave Delilah silver to discover the secret of Samson's strength?
   a. Philistines b. Priests
   c. Scribes d. Amorites

5. For how many pieces of silver was Joseph sold to the Ishmaelites?
   a. 10 b. 20 c. 30 d. 40

6. Who bribed the soldiers to say the disciples had stolen Jesus' body?
   a. Pilate b. the Pharisees
   c. The chief priests d. Herod

7. What was the name of the field bought with the money Judas returned?
   a. Corban b. Golgotha
   c. Akeldama d. Gabbatha

8. Who suggested selling Joseph?
   a. Jacob b. Reuben
   c. Judah d. Benjamin

9. Who hoped that Paul would offer him a bribe to get out of prison?
   a. Felix b. Festus
   c. King Agrippa d. Claudius Lysias

10. Who said to the tax collectors, "Don't collect any more than you are required to"?
    a. Jesus b. Paul
    c. John the Baptist d. Peter

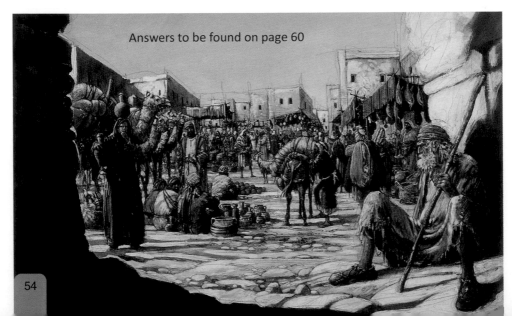

Answers to be found on page 60

Boats in the Bible

1. How long was the ark that Noah built?
    a. 100 metres **b.** 200 inches
    c. 450 feet **d.** 400 yards

2. How many decks did Noah's ark have?
    a. 2 **b.** 3 **c.** 4
    d. None, as it was just one big space

3. Where was the boat headed for that Jonah boarded?
    a. Tarshish **b.** Tunis
    c. Tarsus **d.** Tripoli

4. What was Jesus doing in the boat during the storm on Galilee?
    a. Praying **b.** Sleeping
    c. Bailing water **d.** Steering

5. How many doors did Noah's ark have?
    a. 1 **b.** 2 **c.** 3
    d. None, but a hatch on the roof

6. What cargo was on the ship in which Paul was shipwrecked?
    a. Cedar wood **b.** Oranges
    c. Salted fish **d.** Grain

7. After fourteen days in the storm, what did Paul tell the crew to do?
    a. Pray **b.** Eat some food
    c. Sing **d.** Take to the lifeboats

8. In Paul's shipwreck, how many died?
    a. 5 **b.** 1 **c.** 50 **d.** None

9. Which psalm describes terrified sailors in a fierce storm?
    a. 23 **b.** 119 **c.** 107 **d.** 1

10. When Jonah was in the storm at sea and the captain came to find him, what was Jonah doing?
    a. Praying **b.** Sleeping
    c. Singing **d.** Eating figs

Answers to be found on page 60

What jobs?

1. Who was a mighty hunter?
   a. Nimrod b. Gideon
   c. Goliath d. David

2. Who was a teacher of brass and iron workers?
   a. Jesus b. Tubal-Cain
   c. Jacob d. Solomon

3. What was Luke's profession?
   a. Physician b. Lawyer
   c. Tax collector d. Toymaker

4. What was Paul's craft?
   a. Blacksmith b. Tentmaker
   c. Carpenter d. Fisherman

5. What was Amos' job when God called him to be a prophet?
   a. Shepherd b. Potter
   c. Scribe d. Musician

6. What was Nehemiah's occupation?
   a. Cup-bearer b. Priest
   c. Soldier d. Sailor

7. What was the occupation of David at King Saul's court?
   a. Armour-bearer b. Baker
   c. Steward d. Jester

8. What was the job of the Ethiopian that Philip baptized?
   a. Cup-bearer b. Astrologer
   c. Treasurer d. General

9. What was Zacchaeus' job?
   a. Coach driver b. Tax collector
   c. Bank manager d. Accountant

10. What position did Cornelius hold?
    a. Magistrate b. Admiral
    c. centurion d. High priest

Answers to be found on page 60

Music in the Bible

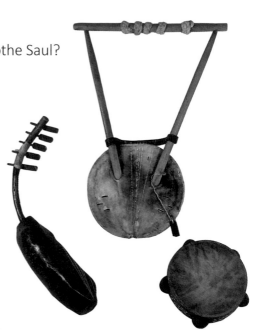

1. What type of instrument did David play to soothe Saul?
   a. Harp b. Horn c. Drums d. Violin

2. What instruments were played when the Ark
   of God came to Jerusalem?
   a. Horns and lyres b. Trumpets and cymbals
   c. Harps d. All of these

3. With what instrument did Miriam lead the
   women out to sing?
   a. Lyres b. Timbrels c. Bagpipes d. Cymbals

4. What instrument does Amos say strikes fear
   into people?
   a. Castanets b. Trumpet c. Cymbals d. Drums

5. Against which army did Gideon's men blow trumpets and shout?
   a. Philistines b. Midianites c. Amalekites d. Samaritans

6. Who was "the father of all who play the harp and flute"?
   a. Jove b. Jupiter c. Tubal d. Jubal

7. Who organized a choir and an orchestra for worship before the Ark
   of the Covenant?
   a. David b. Solomon c. Joash d. Herod

8. In John's vision, what instruments did the seven angels hold?
   a. Harps b. Trumpets c. Horns d. Drums

9. In Jesus' description of a children's game, what instrument did the children play?
   a. Pipe b. Mouth-organ c. Cymbals d. Drum

10. As well as gardens, parks, and other delights, the teacher in Ecclesiastes had a...
    a. String orchestra b. Gospel choir c. Brass band d. Mixed-voice choir

Answers to be found on page 60

Clothes

1. Whose family were clothed in fine linen and purple?
   a. King Solomon's b. Esther's
   c. Job's d. The noble wife's

2. Who tossed dice for a garment too fine to cut up?
   a. Job's comforters b. Paul's jailer
   c. Soldiers at the cross
   d. Joseph's jailer in Egypt

3. Of what animal's hair was John's cloak made?
   a. Sheep b. Camel c. Goat d. Bear

4. What article of clothing did Paul ask for when he was in prison?
   a. Sandals b. Hat c. Cloak d. Tunic

5. When did a teenager escape capture by wriggling out of his clothes?
   a. In the riot in Ephesus
   b. When Jesus was seized
   c. In Philippi with Paul
   d. When Saul and Jonathan died

6. In ancient times, what was taken off and handed over to finalize an agreement?
   a. Belt c. Cloak d. Shawl d. Sandal

7. What was taken off as a sign of reverence for a holy place?
   a. Headgear b. Cloak c. Shoes d. Belt

8. What was Elijah's belt made of?
   a. Silk b. Leather c. Linen d. Wool

9. Who was given a nose ring as a present?
   a. Rebekah b. Ruth
   c. Esther d. Salome

10. Who or what, said Jesus, are dressed more beautifully than Solomon?
    a. Wild flowers b. The Temple
    c. Birds d. Priests

Answers to be found on page 61

Temples, priests, and feasts

1. What did David give Solomon for the Temple?
    a. Gold and silver **b.** Bricks **c.** Candles **d.** Furniture

2. Two pillars in the porch of the Temple were called:
    a. Alpha and Omega **b.** Adam and Eve
    c. Jakin and Boaz **d.** Jacob and Esau

3. What material from Lebanon was used to build Solomon's Temple?
    a. Gold **b.** Cedar wood **c.** Bronze **d.** Concrete

4. Who was the first high priest?
    a. Levi **b.** Aaron **c.** Zadok **c.** We don't know

5. When Jesus threw out the traders, he said that God's house should be a house of . . .
    a. Worship **b.** Prayer **c.** Peace **d.** Truth

6. What was the name of the high priest in Solomon's Temple?
    a. Moses **b.** Zadok **c.** Paul **d.** Herod

7. Who told Pilate that Jesus' tomb should be guarded?
    a. Chief priests and Pharisees **b.** Barabbas
    c. Peter and John **d.** Mary Magdalene

8. On what festival did the priests release the scapegoat?
    a. Passover **b.** Purim
    c. Day of Atonement **d.** Pentecost

9. The Year of Jubilee was celebrated every...
    a. 1 year **b.** 12 years **c.** 100 years **d.** 50 years

10. What is celebrated at Purim?
    a. The Exodus **b.** Israel's deliverance by Esther
    c. Nativity **d.** Harvest

Answers to be found on page 61

Sports and games

1. Run the race marked out for us (Hebrews 12:1)
2. Prize (1 Corinthians 9:24)
3. Weddings and funerals (Luke 7:32)
4. Boxing (1 Corinthians 9:26–27)
5. Samson (Judges 14:12)
6. Dice (John 19:24)
7. Archery (1 Samuel 20:20, 36–37)
8. The second (Exodus 20:4)
9. Jacob (Genesis 32:24–29)
10. The Queen of Sheba (1 Kings 10:1–10)

Food, glorious food!

1. Samson (Judges 14:5–9)
2. Wild gourds (2 Kings 4:38–41)
3. Unleavened (Leviticus 23:4–6)
4. Esau (Genesis 25:29–34)
5. Locusts (Matthew 3:4)
6. Bread (1 Kings 17:10–14)
7. Bread and fish (John 21:9)
8. Manna (Exodus 16:31)
9. Honey (Numbers 13:23)
10. Fig (Matthew 21:19)

Buying, selling, and bribing

1. Ananias (Acts 5:1–2)
2. Amos (Amos 8:5)
3. Simon the sorcerer (Acts 8:18–19)
4. Philistines (Judges 16:5)
5. 20 (Genesis 37:28)
6. The chief priests (Matthew 28:11–15)
7. Akeldama (Acts 1:18–19)
8. Judah (Genesis 37:26–27)
9. Felix (Acts 24:24–26)
10. John the Baptist (Luke 3:13)

Boats in the Bible

1. 450 feet (300 cubits; Genesis 6:15)
2. 3 (Genesis 6:16)
3. Tarshish (Jonah 1:3)
4. Sleeping (Matthew 8:23–27)
5. 1 (Genesis 6:16)
6. Grain (Acts 27:38)
7. Eat some food (Acts 27:33–34)
8. None (Acts 27:44)
9. Psalm 107 (23–30)
10. Sleeping (Jonah 1:5–6)

What jobs?

1. Nimrod (Genesis 10:9)
2. Tubal-Cain (Genesis 4:22)
3. Physician (Colossians 4:14)
4. Tentmaker (Acts 18:2–3)
5. Shepherd (Amos 7:14)
6. Cup-bearer (Nehemiah 2:1)
7. Armour-bearer (1 Samuel 16:21)
8. Treasurer (Acts 8:26–27)
9. Tax collector (Luke 19:2)
10. Centurion (Acts 10:1)

Music in the Bible

1. Harp (1 Samuel 16:23)
2. All of these (1 Chronicles 15:28)
3. Timbrels (Exodus 15:20)
4. Trumpet (Amos 3:6)
5. Midianites (Judges 7:20–23)
6. Jubal (Genesis 4:21)
7. David (1 Chronicles 15:16)
8. Trumpets (Revelation 8:6)
9. Pipe (Luke 7:32)
10. Mixed-voice choir (Ecclesiastes 2:8)

Clothes

1. The noble wife's (Proverbs 31:22)
2. Soldiers at the cross (John 19:23–24)
3. Camel (Matthew 3:4)
4. Cloak (2 Timothy 4:13)
5. When Jesus was seized (Mark 14:51–52)
6. Sandal (Ruth 4:7)
7. Shoes (Joshua 5:15)
8. Leather (2 Kings 1:8)
9. Rebekah (Genesis 24:47)
10. Wild flowers (Matthew 6:28–29)

Temples, priests, and feasts

1. Gold and silver (1 Chronicles 29:3)
2. Jakin and Boaz (1 Kings 7:21)
3. Cedar wood (1 Kings 5:1–10)
4. Aaron (Exodus 28; Leviticus 8)
5. Prayer (Mark 11:17)
6. Zadok (1 Kings 2:27, 35)
7. Chief priests and Pharisees (Matthew 27:62–64)
8. Day of Atonement (Leviticus 16:6–10)
9. 50 years (Leviticus 25:11)
10. Israel's deliverance by Esther (Esther 9:18–32)

Creation and fall

1. On which day of creation did God make humans?
   a. First b. Fourth c. Fifth d. Sixth

2. What did God use to create Adam?
   a. Clay b. Dust of the ground
   c. Water d. Fire

3. Who or what was in the beginning?
   a. God b. Water c. UFOs d. Winter

4. What animal was more crafty than any beast of the field?
   a. Chameleon b. Chipmunk
   c. Serpent d. Parrot

5. What leaves did Adam and Eve use to cover their nakedness?
   a. Fig b. Sycamore c. Tea d. Olive

6. After Adam and Ever sinned, what did God make for them?
   a. Garments of fig leaves
   b. Coats of skins
   c. Skirts made of banana leaves
   d. Linen breeches

7. How many children did Adam and Eve have?
   a. 2 b. 3 c. 4 d. More than 4

8. Who or what did God create on day four?
   a. Humans b. Animals
   c. Plants d. Sun, moon, stars

9. Where did Adam and Eve live before they disobeyed God?
   a. Garden of Gethsemane b. Garden of Eden c. Garden of Delights
   d. Garden of Paradise

10. What was the first thing God created?
    a. Light b. Water c. Fire d. Earth

Answers to be found on page 76

Abraham

1. Where did Abraham (Abram) live with his father after leaving Ur?
   a. Damascus b. Babylon
   c. Haran d. Nineveh

2. What was the name of Abraham's father?
   a. Terah b. Terror c. Isaac d. Laban

3. How old was Abraham when he set out for Canaan?
   a. 50 b. 65 c. 75 d. 100

4. Where did Abraham first build an altar in Canaan?
   a. Shechem b. Bethel c. Ai d. Jebus

5. What relation was Lot to Abraham?
   a. Son b. Nephew
   c. Uncle d. Great-grandson

6. What land did Lot choose when it was time for him to separate from Abraham?
   a. Plain of the Jordan b. Negev
   c. Garden of Eden d. Mount Sinai

7. When Abraham went to Egypt, he said his wife Sarai (Sarah) was his...
   a. Aunt b. Cousin c. Sister d. Friend

8. About which city did Abraham argue with God to prevent its destruction?
   a. Babylon b. Nineveh
   c. Sodom d. Jerusalem

9. Where did Abraham bury Sarah?
   a. Beersheba b. Dead Sea
   c. Cave of Machpelah d. Jerusalem

10. Where was Abraham buried?
    a. Cave of Machpelah b. Negev
    c. Pyramid d. Sodom

Answers to be found on page 76

Jacob and Joseph

1. Who bought Joseph from Midianite traders?
   a. Potiphar b. Pharaoh
   c. Hezekiah d. Prospero

2. What was Joseph called?
   a. The layabout b. The dreamer
   c. The gossiper d. The stargazer

3. What did Joseph's father give to him?
   a. Hat b. Horse c. Bow and arrows
   d. Fancy coat

4. Who dreamed of angels ascending and descending a ladder?
   a. Joseph b. Jacob

5. Joseph's brothers went to Egypt to...
   a. Buy food b. See the pyramids
   c. Buy property d. Find Joseph

6. What name was given to Jacob after he had fought all night with God without letting go?
   a. Judah b. Israel
   c. Peniel d. Mahanaim

7. Into whose bag of grain did Joseph put a silver cup?
   a. Judah's b. Ephraim's
   c. Simeon's d. Benjamin's

8. Who was kept as a hostage to make sure Joseph's brothers returned with Benjamin?
   a. Judah b. Simeon c. Levi d. Gad

9. What was Zaphenath-Paneah's original name?
   a. Joseph b. Jacob c. Benjamin
   d. Ephraim

10. Where was Jacob buried?
    a. In Goshen in Egypt
    b. In Rameses c. In Bethel
    d. In the cave of Machpelah

Answers to be found on page 19

It's all in Genesis

1. What was the first thing Noah built when he left the ark?
   a. Altar b. House c. Church d. Temple

2. How old was Isaac when he married Rebekah?
   a. 20 b. 30 c. 40 d. 50

3. Who was Abraham's first son?
   a. David b. Ishmael c. Isaiah d. Ezekiel

4. What does the name "Eve" mean?
   a. Sly b. Excellent c. Mother of all living d. Argumentative

5. How many times did Noah send the dove from the ark?
   a. 1 b. 2 c. 3 d. 4

6. Esau was…
   a. Lame b. Long-nosed c. Red and hairy d. Pale

7. Who is the oldest person in the Bible?
   a. Enoch b. Mahalaleel c. Abimael d. Methuselah

8. Who was the first person in the Bible to go to heaven without dying?
   a. Enoch b. Elijah c. Shem d. Moses

9. When Lot was captured by the four kings and their armies, Abraham rescued him with how many men?
   a. 318 b. 456 c. 1,000 d. 600

10. After the battle of the kings, to whom did Abraham give a tenth of everything he had?
    a. King of Sodom b. Melchizedek
    c. Lot d. Sarah

Answers to be found on page 76

Moses

1. In which river was Moses hidden among the bulrushes?
   a. Jordan b. Nile
   c. Euphrates d. Ganges

2. Who watched over Moses' basket?
   a. Moses' mother
   b. Miriam, his sister c. Moses' father
   d. Aaron, his brother

3. What did the daughter of Pharaoh do when she saw the basket?
   a. Shrieked b. Ran away
   c. Sent her maid to get it d. Nothing

4. Who was brought to Pharaoh's daughter to nurse the baby?
   a. Her aunt b. Aaron
   c. Her grandmother
   d. The baby's mother

5. What extraordinary sight did Moses see in the desert while he was keeping sheep?
   a. An angel with a sword
   b. A burning bush that didn't burn up c. A donkey that talked
   d. The ghost of Tutankhamun

6. Who told God, "You know I am such a poor speaker; why should the king listen to me?"
   a. Abraham b. Aaron
   c. Moses d. Jacob

7. Who did God say would help Moses?
   a. His mother b. His father
   c. His brother d. His sister

8. What did God want Moses to do?
   a. Rescue the Hebrew people
   b. Help build the pyramids
   c. Confess to the crime of murder
   d. Rule Egypt

9. As God parted the sea for the Israelites, what did Moses hold out over the water?
   a. Cloak b. Hand c. Fish d. Torch

10. Whose bones did Moses take back to Canaan?
    a. Joseph's b. Jacob's c. Abraham's
    d. Aaron's

Answers to be found on page 19

Israelites and the Exodus

1. What city did the Israelites *not* build while slaves in Egypt?
   a. Rameses b. Pithom c. Memphis

2. How many plagues did God send on Egypt?
   a. 7 b. 64 c. 10 d. 250

3. What did Aaron's rod become?
   a. Snake b. Lion c. Spear d. Torch

4. What was the first plague on the Egyptians before the Exodus?
   a. Water turned to blood b. Toads
   c. Snails d. Water turned to wine

5. What sea did the people cross on dry land?
   a. Mediterranean Sea b. Red Sea
   c. Dead Sea d. Sea of Galilee

6. What proportion of his chariots did Pharaoh send after the Hebrews?
   a. A quarter b. Half
   c. Three-quarters d. All

7. What did the Egyptians *not* give to the Hebrews when they left?
   a. Silver
   b. Sheep and goats
   c. Gold d. Clothes

8. Why did Pharoah chase after the Hebrews?
   a. He'd lost his workforce
   b. Revenge for the death of his son
   c. To learn about their God

9. How long were the Israelites in Egypt?
   a. 20 years b. 4,000 years
   c. 430 years d. 5 years

10. What was the feast that celebrated God saving the firstborn children while the people of Israel were in Egypt?
   a. Easter b. Passover
   c. Harvest d. Pentecost

Answers to be found on page 76

Wilderness wanderings

1. Whose punishment for murder was to be "a restless wanderer on the earth"?
   a. Cain **b.** Abel **c.** Moses **d.** David

2. Who, at God's command, set out on a journey without knowing the destination?
   a. Moses **b.** Paul **c.** Nehemiah **d.** Abram

3. Why did Lot and Abram go different ways?
   a. Their servants argued about water and pasture **b.** Their wives argued **c.** Their children argued

4. What did God tell Moses to build in the wilderness?
   a. Church **b.** Synagogue **c.** Tabernacle **d.** Temple

5. A pillar of fire led the Israelites through the wilderness. True or false?

6. Moses said, "The Lord will fight for you, you need only to... "
   a. Pray **b.** Trust **c.** Be still **d.** Work hard

7. Who led the women in a dance after crossing the Red Sea?
   a. Aaron **b.** Miriam **c.** Zipporah **d.** No one

8. When the people were thirsty at Massah and Meribah, how did God supply water?
   a. From a rock **b.** Oasis **c.** Spring **d.** Hosepipe

9. How were the Israelites saved from venomous snakes?
   a. Looking at a bronze snake **b.** Running away **c.** Finding a scapegoat **d.** Building an ark

10. Who gave Moses advice in the desert?
    a. His uncle **b.** His father **c.** His father-in-law **d.** his brother

Answers to be found on page 77

The Ark of the Covenant

1. What was the Ark of the Covenant?
   a. A miniature boat b. A sacred box covered with gold c. A crown
   d. An incredibly holy jewel

2. Which king brought the Ark to Jerusalem?
   a. Saul b. David c. Solomon d. Ahab

3. Who died when he heard that the Ark had been captured?
   a. Solomon b. David c. Eli d. Samuel

4. Where was the Ark kept in Jerusalem?
   a. In the king's palace
   b. In the most holy place of the Temple
   c. In a specially built tent
   d. In the high priest's house

5. To whom did God give instructions to make the Ark?
   a. Samuel b. David
   c. Abraham d. Moses

6. What was in the Ark of the Covenant together with the manna and Aaron's rod?
   a. Golden calf b. Ten Commandments tablets
   c. Holy Grail d. Scriptures

7. Around which city was the Ark of the Covenant carried?
   a. Jericho b. Jerusalem
   c. Cana d. Bethlehem

8. How many gold cherubim were on the Ark of the Covenant?
   a. 1 b. 2 c. 7 d. 144

9. Which Philistine idol fell on its face before the Ark?
   a. Baal b. Diana c. Dagon
   d. Montezuma

10. When did the Ark disappear?
    a. After Solomon died
    b. When the Romans destroyed Jerusalem
    c. Nothing was heard of it after Nebuchadnezzar seized Jerusalem

Answers to be found on page 77

Joshua and Judges

1. What Bible character had long hair that made him strong?
   a. Goliath b. Hezekiah
   c. Samson d. Paul

2. How many times in total did Joshua's army march round the walls of Jericho?
   a. 7 b. 24 c. 13 d. 10

3. Who caught 300 foxes, tied firebrands to their tails, and let them loose in enemies' cornfields?
   a. Abner b. Gideon
   c. Samson d. Gilead

4. Who was the thief who caused the Israelites to lose the battle for Ai?
   a. Ananias
   b. Achan
   c. Issachar
   d. Salumna

5. Which judge defeated a huge army with only 300 men?
   a. Deborah b. Gideon
   c. Samson d. Ehud

6. Which judge of Israel destroyed the temple of Dagon?
   a. Gideon b. Othniel
   c. Shamgar d. Samson

7. What did Joshua set up in the middle of the river Jordan after crossing?
   a. Statue b. Altar
   c. Dam d. Twelve stones

8. What did the Israelites ask Samuel for?
   a. An emperor b. A king
   c. A pharaoh d. A chief priest

9. To which tribe of Israel did Ehud belong?
   a. Simeon b. Benjamin
   c. Judah d. Asher

10. Which judge sat under a palm tree between Ramah and Bethel?
    a. Othniel
    b. Ehud
    c. Deborah
    d. Gideon

Answers to be found on page 77

Spies, plots, and disguises

1. Why did King Saul put on a disguise?
   a. To escape his enemies
   b. To go to a party
   c. To trap David
   d. To see a witch secretly

2. In what town did Rahab hide spies on her roof?
   a. Jerusalem b. Jericho c. Egypt
   d. Babylon

3. The Gibeonites wore travel-worn clothes and carried mouldy bread to persuade Joshua that they couldn't fight because they...
   a. Were too poor
   b. Lived too far away
   c. Were too weak

4. Jacob dressed up to smell and feel like Esau to get Esau's...
   a. Dog b. Blessing from his father
   c. Wife d. Money

5. Why did Joseph's brothers not recognize Joseph in Egypt?
   a. He was dressed as a shepherd
   b. He was dressed as a trader
   c. He was dressed as an Egyptian leader
   d. He was dressed as a pirate

6. When David fled form Absalom, who stayed on in Absalom's court as a spy?
   a. Jonathan b. Micha
   c. Hushai d. Nathan

7. Which king went to battle disguised as an ordinary soldier?
   a. Ahab b. David
   c. Jehoshaphat d. Jehu

8. Who tricked some king's men by disguising an idol to look like her husband asleep in bed?
   a. Deborah b. Michal
   c. Abigail d. Jezebel

9. How many spies did Moses send into the Promised Land?
   a. 8 b. 10 c. 12 d. 14

10. What did David pretend to be before King Achish?
    a. A poor man
    b. A mad man
    c. A sick man
    d. A rich man

Answers to be found on page 77

David and Goliath

1. How many sons did Jesse have?
   a. 8 b. 7 c. 10 d. 24

2. When his brothers went to war, David looked after his father's...
   a. Corn b. Sheep c. Cows d. Vines

3. David went to the battle lines to take his brothers some...
   a. Food b. Money c. Clothes d. Books

4. Whose champion fighter was Goliath?
   a. Philistines b. Phoenicians
   c. Egyptians d. Romans

5. Goliath was over 9 feet (2.75 metres) tall.
   True or false?

6. For how many days did Goliath challenge Israel to send a man to fight him?
   a. 2 days b. 365 days c. 40 days
   d. 750 days

7. What did David not take into battle?
   a. Sling b. Helmet d. Five smooth stones d. Shepherd's bag

8. How many stones did David put in his shepherd's bag when he set out towards Goliath?
   a. 7 b. 5 c. 12 d. 1

9. What did David use to kill Goliath?
   a. Sword b. Spear c. Gun d. Sling

10. Where did David's stone hit Goliath?
    a. Forehead b. Chest c. Arm d. Leg

Answers to be found on page 77

King David and sons

1. Who condemned David for his affair with Bathsheba?
   a. Balaam b. Nathan c. Nabal
   d. Elijah

2. Who did David marry after her husband died of a stroke?
   a. Abigail b. Michal c. Maacah
   d. Bathsheba

3. Which of David's sons rebelled and seized the throne?
   a. Amnon b. Adonijah c. Absalom
   d. Solomon

4. How many men joined David when he was an outlaw?
   a. 50 b.100 c. 450 d. 600

5. Which of these was not in Solomon's Temple?
   a. Baptistery b. Lampstands
   c. Ark of the Covenant
   d. Cherubim

6. Solomon had 700 wives. True or false?

7. Why was God angry with Solomon?
   a. He had too many wives
   b. He followed other gods
   c. He did not keep the Sabbath
   d. He did not build a temple

8. What did Solomon do that the people hated?
   a. Built the Temple
   b. Married hundreds of women
   c. Imposed heavy taxes
   d. Did not engage in wars

9. Which king threatened to cut a baby in half?
   a. Ahab b. Saul c. Solomon d. David

10. Which was David's capital city before Jerusalem?
   a. Shiloh
   b. Bethlehem
   c. Bethel
   d. Hebron

Answers to be found on page 78

Lives of the prophets

1. Which of these was thrown into the fiery furnace?
   a. Peniel b. Daniel
   c. Samuel d. Abednego

2. Who built an altar, put a sacrifice on it, ordered it to be drenched with water, and then called to God who then sent fire from heaven?
   a. Moses b. Aaron c. Elijah d. Elisha

3. Who saved 100 prophets from Jezebel by hiding them in a cave?
   a. Elijah b. Elisha c. Nabal d. Obadiah

4. Which woman had a room built on to the house so Elisha could stay?
   a. Miriam b. Michal
   c. Milcah d. She isn't named

5. Why was Jonah thrown into the sea?
   a. He was rude to the sailors
   b. He had stolen some jewels
   c. To feed a big fish
   d. It was the only way to save the ship

6. What was Elisha doing when Elijah threw his cloak over him?
   a. Fishing b. Praying
   c. Ploughing d. Sleeping

7. Which prophet foretold that Jesus would be born in Bethlehem?
   a. Malachi b. Micah
   c. Isaiah d. Ezekiel

8. Who said, "how long will you waver between two opinions? If the Lord is God, follow him"?
   a. Isaiah b. Moses
   c. Elijah d. Jeremiah

9. Where can you read about the valley full of dry bones that came together and came alive?
   a. Isaiah b. Jeremiah
   c. Ezekiel d. Daniel

10. Who told Naaman about the prophet Elisha?
    a. The king b. Wife
    c. An Israelite servant girl d. A butler

Answers to be found on page 78

All in the Old Testament

1. Whose last act before she died was to put make-up on her eyes and redo her hair?
   a. Deborah c. Jezebel c. Miriam d. Esther

2. Who refused to appear before her husband, the king?
   a. Esther b. Vashti c. Queen of Sheba d. Queen Candace

3. Which priest stayed loyal to David and anointed Solomon?
   a. Nathan b. Zadok c. Ittai d. Levi

4. Who collected leftover grain from the edge of a field?
   a. Sarah b. Mary c. Miriam d. Ruth

5. Which king "from his shoulders" was taller than any of the people?
   a. Solomon b. David c. Saul d. Samson

6. Whose patience is famous?
   a. James b. Job c. Jesse d. Isaac

7. Which king took the Israelites captive in Babylon?
   a. Meshach b. Belshazzar c. Nebuchadnezzar d. Cyrus

8. Which of these men was Esther's cousin?
   a. Hosea b. Xerxes c. Mordecai d. Haman

9. Artazerxes was king of...
   a. Persia b. Babylon c. Israel d. Judah

10. Who was terrified by the writing on the wall?
    a. David b. Herod c. Daniel d. Belshazzar

Answers to be found on page 78

ANSWERS

Creation and fall

1. Sixth (Genesis 1:24–31)
2. Dust of the ground (Genesis 2:7)
3. God (Genesis 1:1)
4. Serpent (Genesis 3:1)
5. Fig (Genesis 3:7)
6. Coats of skins (Genesis 2:21)
7. More than 4 (Genesis 5:4)
8. Sun, moon, stars (Genesis 1:14)
9. Garden of Eden (Genesis 2:8)
10. Light (Genesis 1:3)

Abraham

1. Haran (Genesis 11:31)
2. Terah (Genesis 11;27)
3. 75 (Genesis 12:4)
4. Shechem (Genesis 12: 6–7)
5. Nephew (Genesis 14:12)
6. Plain of the Jordan (Genesis 13:11)
7. Sister (Genesis 12:13)
8. Sodom (Genesis 18:16–33)
9. Cave of Machpelah (Genesis 23:19)
10. Cave of Machpelah (Genesis 25:8–10)

Jacob and Joseph

1. Potiphar (Genesis 37:36)
2. The dreamer (Genesis 37:19)
3. Fancy coat (Genesis 37:3)
4. Jacob (Genesis 28:10–12)
5. Buy food (Genesis 52:2)
6. Israel (Genesis 32:28)
7. Benjamin's (Genesis 44:12)
8. Simeon (Genesis 42:24)
9. Joseph (Genesis 41:45)
10. In the cave of Machpelah (Genesis 50:13)

It's all in Genesis

1. Altar (Genesis 8:18–20)
2. 40 (Genesis 25:20)
3. Ishmael (Genesis 16:1–11, 15)
4. Mother of all living (Genesis 3:20)
5. 3 (Genesis 8:8–12)
6. Red and hairy (Genesis 25:25)
7. Methuselah (Genesis 5:27)
8. Enoch (Genesis 5;24; Hebrews 11:5)
9. 318 (Genesis 14:14)
10. Melchizedek (Genesis 14:18–20)

Moses

1. Nile (Exodus 2:1–10)
2. Miriam, his sister (Exodus 2:4)
3. Sent her maid to get it (Exodus 2:5)
4. The baby's mother (Exodus 2:8)
5. A burning bush that didn't burn up (Exodus 3:2)
6. Moses (Exodus 6:30)
7. His brother (Exodus 4:14)
8. Rescue the Hebrew people (Exodus 3:10)
9. Hand (Exodus 14:21)
10. Joseph's (Exodus 13:19)

Israelites and the Exodus

1. Memphis (Exodus 1:11)
2. 10 (Exodus 7–11)
3. Snake (Exodus 7:8–12)
4. Water turned to blood (Exodus 7:17–20)
5. Red Sea (Sea of Reeds, Exodus 13:18–24:22)
6. All (Exodus 14:9)
7. Sheep and goats (Exodus 12:35)
8. He's lost his workforce (Exodus 14:5)
9. 430 years (Exodus 12:40–41)
10. Passover (Exodus 12:27)

Wilderness wanderings

1. Cain (Genesis 4:13–14)
2. Abram (Genesis 12:1)
3. Their servants argued about water and pasture (Genesis 13)
4. Tabernacle (Exodus 25:8–9)
5. False, it was a pillar of cloud (Exodus 13:21)
6. Be still (Exodus 14:14)
7. Miriam (Exodus 15:20)
8. From a rock (Exodus 17:2–7)
9. Looking at a bronze snake (Numbers 21:8–9)
10. His father-in-law (Exodus 18)

The Ark of the Covenant

1. A sacred box covered with gold (Exodus 25:10–22)
2. David (2 Samuel 6:1–17)
3. Eli (1 Samuel 4:10–18)
4. In the most holy place of the Temple (1 Kings 8:6)
5. Moses (Exodus 25:1, 10–22)
6. Ten Commandments tablets (Hebrews 9:4)
7. Jericho (Joshua 6:1–20)
8. 2 (Exodus 37:7)
9. Dagon (1 Samuel 5:3)
10. Nothing is heard of it after Nebuchadnezzar seized Jerusalem (2 Kings 24:8–17; 25:1–15)

Joshua and Judges

1. Samson (Judges 16:4–21)
2. 13 (once each day for six days and then 7 times on the seventh day; Joshua 6:3–4)
3. Samson (Judges 15:1–8)
4. Achan (Joshua 7:20–22)
5. Gideon (Judges 7:7)
6. Samson (Judges 16:23–30)
7. Twelve stones (Joshua 4:9)
8. A king (1 Samuel 8:4–5)
9. Benjamin (Judges 3:15)
10. Deborah (Judges 4:4–5)

Spies, plots, and disguises

1. To see a witch secretly (1 Samuel 28:7–8)
2. Jericho (Joshua 2:6)
3. Lived too far away (Joshua 9)
4. Blessing from his father (Genesis 27)
5. He was dressed as an Egyptian leader (Genesis 42:8)
6. Hushai (2 Samuel 15:32–37)
7. Ahab (1 Kings 22:29–36)
8. Michal (1 Samuel 19:11–16)
9. 12 (Numbers 13:1–15)
10. A mad man (1 Samuel 21:13)

David and Goliath

1. 8 (1 Samuel 17:12)
2. Sheep (1 Samuel 17:15)
3. Food (1 Samuel 17:17)
4. Philistines (1 Samuel 17:4)
5. True (over 6 cubits 1 Samuel 17:4)
6. 40 days (1 Samuel 17:16)
7. Helmet (1 Samuel 17:38–40)
8. 5 (1 Samuel 17:40)
9. Sling (1 Samuel 17:49)
10. Forehead (1 Samuel 17:49)

King David and sons

1. Nathan (2 Samuel 12:1–15)
2. Abigail (1 Samuel 25:36–42)
3. Absalom (2 Samuel 15)
4. 600 (1 Samuel 23:13)
5. Baptistery
6. True (1 Kings 11:1–3)
7. He followed other gods
   (1 Kings 11:9–10)
8. Imposed heavy taxes (1 Kings 12:3–4)
9. Solomon (1 Kings 3:16–27)
10. Hebron (2 Samuel 5:5)

Lives of the prophets

1. Abednego (Daniel 3:22–23)
2. Elijah (1 Kings 18:30–39)
3. Obadiah (1 Kings 18:3–4)
4. She isn't named (2 Kings 4:8–10)
5. It was the only way to save the ship
   (Jonah 1:11–15)
6. Ploughing (1 Kings 19:19)
7. Micah (Micah 5:2)
8. Elijah (1 Kings 18:21)
9. Ezekiel (Ezekiel 37:1–10)
10. An Israelite servant girl (2 Kings 5:2–4)

All in the Old Testament

1. Jezebel (2 Kings 9:30–33)
2. Vashti (Esther 1:12)
3. Zadok (1 Kings 1:32–40)
4. Ruth (Ruth 2:2–3)
5. Saul (1 Samuel 9:2)
6. Job (James 5:11)
7. Nebuchadnezzar (2 Kings 25)
8. Mordecai (Esther 2:7)
9. Persia (Ezra 7:1)
10. Belshazzar (Daniel 5:8–12)

Nativity quiz

How well do you know the Nativity story?

1. How many wise men were there?
   a. 3 b. 4 c. The Bible doesn't say d. 7

2. Did Joseph meet the wise men?
   a. Yes b. No c. The Bible doesn't say

3. What animal did Mary ride to Bethlehem?
   a. Donkey b. Small horse c. Llama d. The Bible doesn't say

4. What sort of building was Jesus born in?
   a. Stable b. Cave d. Inn d. The Bible doesn't say

5. The wise men followed the star from the East to Jerusalem. True or false?

6. The angels sang, "Glory to God in the highest and peace to people on earth."
   True or false?

7. Who was the angel that spoke to John's father?
   a. Michael b. Gabriel c. None did d. Lucifer

Answers to be found on page 90

8. In the Temple, what did Simeon tell Mary would pierce her soul?
   a. An arrow b. Joy c. A sword d. A flame

9. Who, besides the wise men, saw the star?
   a. The shepherds b. King Herod
   c. Herod's astrologers
   d. The Bible doesn't say

10. How did the star compare in brightness with the other stars?
    a. Brighter b. The same
    c. the Bible doesn't say
    d. Not so bright

A king is born

1. Who was promised he would not see death before he had seen baby Jesus?
   a. Zechariah b. Joseph
   c. Simeon d. John the Baptist

2. Who was Mary's cousin's husband?
   a. Zadok b. Zedekiah
   c. Zebedee d. Zechariah

3. Who was the mother of John the Baptist?
   a. Sarah b. Elizabeth
   c. Anna d. Salome

4. What did Mary do right after the angel appeared to her?
   a. Visited Elizabeth
   b. Married Joseph
   c. Went to Bethlehem
   d. Went to Jerusalem

5. Who was the king of Judea at the time of the birth of Jesus?
   a. Herod b. Pilate c. Caesar d. David

6. What was the name of the prophetess who saw the baby Jesus in the Temple?
   a. Huldah b. Anna
   c. Miriam d. We don't know

7. How old was the prophetess who saw Jesus in the Temple?
   a. 54 b. 64 c. 74 d. 84

8. Which was not a gift the wise men brought to Jesus?
   a. Myrrh b. Frankincense
   c. Silver d. Gold

9. Where did Joseph take his family to escape form Herod?
   a. Nazareth b. Egypt
   c. Bethlehem d. The East

10. The word "magi" means "wise men". They were:
    a. Kings b. Astrologers
    c. Magicians d. Magistrates

Answers to be found on page 90

Peter, James, and John

1. What was Peter's other name?
   a. Simon b. Simeon
   c. Samuel d. Samson

2. Which two disciples did Jesus take up the mountain with Peter when he was transfigured?
   a. Matthew and Nathaniel
   b. James and John
   c. Paul and Silas d. Thomas and Andrew

3. Who appeared on the mountain of the transfiguration?
   a. Elijah and Elisha
   b. Moses and Elijah
   c. Moses and Aaron d. Angels

4. Who was the father of James and John?
   a. Zechariah b. Zerubbabel
   c. Zacchaeus d. Zebedee

5. What were James and John doing when Jesus called them?
   a. Fishing b. Begging
   c. Mending tents d. Singing

6. What was the relationship of James and John to Peter?
   a. Cousins b. Business partners
   c. Friends d. Brothers

7. Complete Jesus' words: "You are Peter and on this... I will build my church."
   a. Faith b. Life c. Servant d. Rock

8. Who did Peter and John heal by the Beautiful Gate?
   a. Blind man b. Lame man
   c. Leper d. Deaf man

9. Who wrote the fourth book of the New Testament?
   a. Mark b. John c. Matthew d. Luke

10. Who, apart form Jesus, tried to walk on water?
    a. John b. Jonah c. Peter d. James

Answers to be found on page 90

Why?

1. Why did Judas kiss Jesus?

2. Why did Peter cry?

3. Why did Saul go along the Damascus road?

4. Why did four men climb through a roof?

5. Why did Jesus eat fish on the first Easter?

6. Why did Peter and John follow a man with a water jar?

7. Why did Jesus get a towel and bowl of water?

8. Why did the disciples wake up Jesus?

9. Why did Jesus praise a poor widow?

10. Why did Paul and Silas not escape from prison?

Answers to be found on page 90

Who?

1. Who jumped into the sea when he saw the risen Jesus?
   a. Luke b. Matthew c. Peter d. Noah

2. Who discovered Jesus was missing from the tomb?
   a. Maria b. Mary Magdalene c. Martha d. Maggie

3. Who was the silversmith in Ephesus who incited a riot?
   a. Dionysius b. Demas c. Demetrius d. Artemis

4. Who asked Herod for the head of John the Baptist?
   a. Herodias b. Salome, the daughter of Herodias c. Sapphira d. Candace

5. Who is described as small in height?
   a. Jeremiah b. Zacchaeus c. Paul d. Noah

6. Who was the businesswoman in Philippi who became a Christian?
   a. Damaris b. Dorcas c. Lydia d. Syntyche

7. Who was the member of the Areopagus in Athens who became a Christian?
   a. Dionysius b. Demetrius c. Andronicus d. Urbanus

8. Who bound his hands and feet to warn Paul?
   a. Agabus b. Julius c. Apollos d. Silas

9. Who was Timothy's mother?
   a. Rhoda b. Lois c. Eunice d. Lydia

10. Who was the learned Christian who came from Alexandria and watered the seed that Paul planted?
    a. Apollos b. Aquila c. Ananias d. Luke

Answers to be found on page 91

The Apostle Paul

1. Paul (Saul) was present for the stoning of which early disciple of Christ?
   a. James b. Ananias
   c. Stephen d. Peter

2. Who did God tell to heal Paul when he was blind?
   a. Dr Luke b. Barnabas
   c. Ananias c. Aquila

3. Who did people at Lystra think Barnabas and Paul were?
   a. Moses and Elijah b. Gabriel and Michael c. Zeus and Hermes
   d. John and Jesus

4. In which city did Paul speak to a meeting of the Areopagus?
   a. Rome b. Athens
   c. Antioch d. Corinth

5. At Troas, where Paul set sail for Europe, who was he joined by?
   a. Timothy b. Barnabas
   c. Luke d. Titus

6. When the Jews in Damascus plotted to kill Paul, how did he escape?
   a. Disguised as a woman
   b. Under boxes in a cart
   c. In a basket lowered from a wall
   d. In a great fish

7. Who overheard a plot to kill Paul in Jerusalem?
   a. Luke b. Mark c. Paul's nephew
   d. Paul's mother

8. In which town did sorcerers who had become Christians make a public bonfire of all their scrolls?
   a. Corinth b. Rome
   c. Ephesus d. Athens

9. Before he was a Christian, Paul was proud of being a …
   a. Pharisee b. Lawyer
   c. Sadducee d. Priest

10. Who was the centurion who saved Paul's life in a shipwreck?
    a. Julius b. Festus
    c. Cornelius d. We don't know

Answers to be found on page 91

The first Christians

1. Where did Jesus tell the apostles to go to wait for the Holy Spirit?
   a. Jerusalem b. Bethany
   c. Sea of Galilee d. Capernaum

2. What did Paul encourage Timothy to drink?
   a. Milk b. Wine
   c. Grape juice d. Beer

3. Which apostle was stoned but survived?
   a. Peter b. James c. Stephen d. Paul

4. On which day did the Holy Spirit rest on the apostles in tongues of fire?
   a. Purim b. Pentecost
   c. Easter d. Passover

5. Where were the believers first called "Christians"?
   a. Bethlehem b. Antioch
   c. Jerusalem d. Athens

6. How many people believed after Peter's sermon on the Day of Pentecost?
   a. 3 b. 30 c. 300 d. 3,000

7. On the road from Jerusalem to Gaza, Philip talked to an official from which country?
   a. Egypt b. Persia
   c. Ethiopia d. Arabia

8. In Peter's vision of a large sheet with many animals on it, God was teaching him...
   a. To be kind to animals
   b. To eat all kinds of food
   c. To accept people of all nations
   d. To levitate

9. Which of the named brothers of Jesus became an apostle?
   a. Jude b. James c. Jeremiah d. José

10. The angel told Cornelius to send for Peter, who was staying with...
    a. Dorcas b. Aeneas
    c. Simon the tanner
    d. Philip the deacon

Answers to be found on page 91

The Acts of the Apostles

1. On the Day of Pentecost, the disciples heard the sound of a great...
    a. Sea **b.** Crowd **c.** Wind **d.** Hooter

2. In what did the disciples see Jesus taken to heaven?
    a. Chariot **b.** Cloud **c.** Whirlwind **d.** Hurricane

3. Acts is the fourth book of the New Testament. True or false?

4. On the Day of Pentecost, what did the disciples see over each of their heads?
    a. Rose **b.** Sword **c.** Flame of fire **d.** Cup of wine

5. The first believers shared everything they had.
    True or false?

6. Who was thrown into prison by Herod but then saved by an angel?
    a. John **b.** Peter **c.** James **d.** John the Baptist

7. The book of Acts was written by...
    a. Luke **b.** Moses **c.** Peter **d.** Paul

8. The book of Acts starts in Jerusalem. Where does it end?
    a. In Jerusalem **b.** In Rome
    c. In India **d.** In Spain

9. When Paul was going to Damascus, who did he see in a great light?
    a. Moses **b.** No one
    c. Jesus **d.** An angel

10. After Paul saw the light, he could not...
    a. See **b.** Speak **d.** Walk **d.** Hear

Answers to be found on page 91

What's in the letter?

1. In 2 Corinthians, what kind of giver does God love?
   a. Generous b. Prompt
   c. Regular d. Cheerful

2. According to his letter to the Galatians, what was Paul's main mission from God?
   a. To love everyone
   b. To set up a hotel
   c. To preach among the Gentiles

3. What was Paul collecting for the Jerusalem church?
   a. Clothes b. Money
   c. Food d. Furniture

4. When writing about being justified by faith, Paul uses the example of David and one other Old Testament figure. Who is it?
   a. Noah b. Abraham
   c. Moses d. Jacob

5. Which two people also write the letters to the Thessalonians with Paul?
   a. James and John
   b. Peter and Mark
   c. Silvanus and Timothy
   d. Barnabas and Silas

6. Which of the following is not in the list of things Paul urges the Thessalonians to do at the end of his first letter?
   a. Eat healthily b. Pray continually
   c. Rejoice always
   d. Give thanks in all circumstances

7. According to his letter to the Ephesians, how many pieces of spiritual armour are there?
   a. 4 b. 6 c. 8 d. 10

8. According to James, what does the testing of faith produce?
   a. Joy b. Riches
   c. Perseverance d. Patience

9. What does Peter warn about in his second letter?
   a. False teachers b. Spiteful words
   c. Tripping hazards d. Viruses

10. Who is the third letter of John written to?
    a. James b. Jude
    c. Philemon d. Gaius

Answers to be found on page 91

All in the New Testament

1. Which was not one of Satan's temptations of Jesus?
   a. Changing stones into bread b. Worshipping the devil
   c. Jumping off the Temple d. Walking on water

2. The Greek woman from Syro-Phoenica said, "Even the... under the table eat the children's food."
   a. Chickens b. Dogs c. Ants d. Mice

3. What secret sign were Peter and John to look out for in Jerusalem?
   a. A man with a woman's umbrella b. A woman with a rose
   c. A man with a water jar d. A woman with a towel

4. Who was the girl who opened the door to Peter after he escaped from prison?
   a. Rhoda b. Euodia c. Lydia d. Priscilla

5. From whom did Jesus cast out seven devils?
   a. A man called Legion b. Salome
   c. Mary Magdalene d. The lame man

Answers to be found on page 91

6. How many apostles did Jesus choose?
   a. 7 b. 4 c. 10 d. 12

7. Who, in the course of many journeys, was shipwrecked three times?
   a. Moses b. Peter c. Paul d. Jonah

8. On which island was John imprisoned for preaching?
   a. Cyprus b. Patmos c. Crete d. Sicily

9. In Revelation, the streets in the new Jerusalem are made of what?
   a. Myrrh b. Asphalt c. Gold d. Diamonds

10. According to Revelation, where will the last great battle take place?
    a. Jerusalem b. Damascus c. Armageddon d. Mars

ANSWERS

Nativity quiz

1. The Bible doesn't say
2. The Bible doesn't say. Matthew writes that the magi found the child with Mary (Matthew 2:9–11)
3. The Bible doesn't say (Luke 2:4–6)
4. The Bible doesn't say. Luke writes that the baby was placed in a manger (Luke 2:6–8)
5. False. They saw the star in the east and assumed the king would be born in Jerusale (Matthew 2:1–11)
6. False. The angels sang, "... and on earth peace to those on whom God's favour rests" (Luke 2:14)
7. Gabriel (Luke 1:19)
8. A sword (Luke 2:35)
9. The Bible doesn't say
10. The Bible doesn't say

A king is born

1. Simeon (Luke 2:25–26)
2. Zechariah (Luke 1:5, 36)
3. Elizabeth (Luke 1:38–40)
4. Visited Elizabeth (Luke 1:38–40)
5. Herod (Matthew 2:1)
6. Anna (Luke 2:36)
7. 85 (Luke 2:37)
8. Silver (Matthew 2:11)
9. Egypt (Matthew 2:13–15)
10. Astrologers

Peter, James, and John

1. Simon (Matthew 4:18)
2. James and John (Matthew 17:1–2)
3. Moses and Elijah (Matthew 17:3)
4. Zebedee (Matthew 4:21)
5. Fishing (Luke 5:1–11)
6. Business partners in fishing (Luke 5:10)
7. Rock (Matthew 16:18)
8. Lame man (Acts 3:1–10)
9. John
10. Peter (Matthew 14:29)

Why?

1. To show the guards who Jesus was (Matthew 26:48–49)
2. Because he had denied knowing Jesus three times (Matthew 26:75)
3. To arrest Christians (Acts 9:1–3)
4. The house was too full, and they wanted to get their paralyzed friend to Jesus (Mark 2:1–4)
5. To show he was not a ghost (Luke 24:39–43)
6. To find where to go to prepare the Passover meal (Mark 14:13–15)
7. To wash his disciples' feet (John 13)
8. Their boat was in a violent storm (Luke 8:24)
9. She had put all the money she had in the Temple collecting box (Luke 21:4)
10. So the jailer would not be in trouble and would believe (Acts 16:27–31)

Who?

1. Peter (John 21:7)
2. Mary Magdalene (John 20:1)
3. Demetrius (Acts 19:23–29)
4. Salome, the daughter of Herodias (Mark 6:21–28)
5. Zacchaeus (Luke 19:2–4)
6. Lydia (Acts 16:14)
7. Dionysius (Acts 17:34)
8. Agabus (Acts 21:10–14)
9. Eunice (2 Timothy 1:5)
10. Apollos (Acts 18:24–26; 1 Corinthians 3:6)

The Apostle Paul

1. Stephen (Acts 7:58)
2. Ananias (Acts 9:12)
3. Zeus and Hermes (Acts 14:11–12)
4. Athens (Acts 17:16, 19)
5. Luke (Acts 16:11)
6. In a basket lowered from a wall (Acts 9:25)
7. Paul's nephew (Acts 23:12–16)
8. Ephesus (Acts 19:17–19)
9. Pharisee (Philippians 3:5–6)
10. Julius (Acts 27:1, 42–43)

The first Christians

1. Jerusalem (Luke 24:49)
2. Wine (1 Timothy 5:23)
3. Paul (Acts 14:19–20)
4. Pentecost (Acts 2:1–3)
5. Antioch (Acts 11:26)
6. 3,000 (Acts 2:41)
7. Ethiopia (Acts 8:27)
8. To accept people of all nations (Acts 10:9–28)
9. James (Galatians 1:19)
10. Simon the tanner (Acts 10:32)

The Acts of the Apostles

1. Wind (Acts 2:2)
2. Cloud (Acts 1:9)
3. False: it's the fifth book
4. Flame of fire (Acts 2:3)
5. True (Acts 4:32)
6. Peter (Acts 12:1–10)
7. Luke
8. In Rome (Acts 28:16–31)
9. Jesus (Acts 9:3–7)
10. See (Acts 9:8)

What's in the letter?

1. Cheerful (2 Corinthians 9:7)
2. To preach among the Gentiles (Galatians 1:16)
3. Money (Romans 15:25–26)
4. Abraham (Romans 4:1–8)
5. Silvanus and Timothy (1 Thessalonians 1:1)
6. Eat healthily (1 Thessalonians 5:16–18)
7. 6 (Ephesians 6:13–17)
8. Perseverance (James 1:3)
9. False teachers (2 Peter 2:1)
10. Gaius (3 John:1)

All in the New Testament

1. Walking on water (Matthew 4:1–10)
2. Dogs (Mark 7:28)
3. A man with a water jar (Luke 22:8–10)
4. Rhoda (Acts 12:13–14)
5. Mary Magdalene (Mark 16:9)
6. 12 (Luke 6:12–16)
7. Paul (2 Corinthians 11:25)
8. Patmos (Revelation 1:9)
9. Gold (Revelation 21:21)
10. Armageddon (Revelation 16:16)

The Christmas quiz

1. In which town was Jesus born?

2. Who was Jesus' mother?

3. What was Jesus wrapped in when he was born?

4. Where was baby Jesus laid when he was born?

5. How did the shepherds know Jesus had been born?

6. What did the shepherds do after seeing baby Jesus?

7. How did the wise men know there was a new king?

8. What gifts did the wise men bring?

9. Why did Joseph have to take Jesus and his mother to Egypt?

10. How long did they have to stay in Egypt?

Answers to be found on page 102

The Jesus quiz part 1

1. Where was Jesus presented as a baby?

2. Where did Jesus grow up?

3. Where did Mary and Joseph lose Jesus as a boy?

4. What was Jesus' job in Nazareth?

5. Which fishermen were mending their nets when Jesus called them to be disciples?

6. Jesus was tempted in the wilderness: how many temptations were written about?

7. What did Jesus eat when he was in the wilderness for forty days?

8. Where was Jesus walking when he called his first disciples?

9. What do we call the stories Jesus told?

10. At what age did Jesus begin his ministry?

Answers to be found on page 102

Miracles

1. How many water pots were filled when Jesus turned water into wine?

2. What happened to the evil spirits Jesus cast out of Legion?

3. When Jesus healed ten lepers, how many said thank you?

4. When Jesus healed a blind man, the man said at first, "The people look like… walking."

5. What did the woman in the crowd touch to be healed?

6. After four friends brought a paralyzed man to Jesus, what did Jesus tell him to pick up before going home?

7. To whom or to what was Jesus speaking when he said, "Peace, be still"?

8. What did Jesus tell the disciples to do when they caught no fish?

9. Why did the synagogue leader complain when Jesus healed a woman, who could *not* stand straight?

10. Why was Jesus amazed at the centurion, whose servant he healed?

Answers to be found on page 102

The Jesus quiz part 2

1. What does "Emmanuel" mean?
   a. Jesus b. Saviour
   c. Man of God d. God with us

2. In which river was Jesus baptized?
   a. Jordan b. Nile
   c. Rhine d. Euphrates

3. Who came to see Jesus at night?
   a. Nathanael b. Jairus
   c. Nicodemus
   d. Joseph of Arimathea

4. What town did Jesus make his base?
   a. Nazareth b. Jerusalem
   c. Caesarea d. Capernaum

5. What did God say at Jesus' baptism?
   a. "Go and do likewise"
   b. "Behold, the Lamb of God"
   c. "This is my beloved Son"
   d. "Hallelujah"

6. At which festival did the twelve-year-old Jesus stay behind at the Temple?
   a. Purim b. Christmas
   c. Passover d. Pentecost

7. What is the name of the Pharisee who invited Jesus for a meal?
   a. Nicodemus b. Gamaliel
   c. Simon d. We don't know

8. Who did Jesus eat with when he was in Jericho?
   a. Matthew b. Zacchaeus
   c. Joseph of Arimathea
   d. Nicodemus

9. Whom did Jesus call a "brood of vipers"?
   a. Romans b. Thieves
   c. Scorpions d. Pharisees

10. To whom did Jesus say, "Get behind me, Satan"?
    a. John the Baptist b. Peter
    c. Judas d. A Pharisee

Answers to be found on page 102

Gospel queries

1. Which parable of Jesus is only in John's Gospel?
   a. Talents b. Good shepherd
   c. Fig tree d. Ten bridesmaids

2. At which pool did Jesus heal a man who had been ill for thirty-eight years?
   a. Beautiful b. Bethesda
   c. Siloam d. Galilee

3. Apart from "The Word", who is the first person mentioned in John's Gospel?
   a. John the Baptist b. James
   c. Luke d. Mary

4. Who of the following is mentioned only in John's Gospel?
   a. Nicodemus b. Paul
   c. Zacchaeus d. Martha

5. By whose well did Jesus sit down in Samaria?
   a. David's b. Joseph's
   c. Jacob's d. Saul's

6. What miracle is told only in Luke's Gospel?
   a. Water into wine
   b. Healing of ten lepers
   c. Feeding of the five thousand
   d. Resurrection

7. Where did Jesus tell a blind man to wash?
   a. River Jordan b. Pool of Siloam
   c. Sea of Galilee d. Pool of Bethesda

8. What post did Pontius Pilate hold?
   a. Chief priest b. King
   c. Governor d. Magistrate

9. What did Pilate do when sentencing Jesus to death?
   a. Clapped b. Washed his hands
   c. Cheered d. Drank some wine

10. What happened to the Temple curtain when Jesus died?
    a. Pulled down b. Caught fire
    c. Blown away d. Torn in two

Answers to be found on page 102

More Gospel stories

1. When four friends carried a paralyzed man to Jesus, how did they get into the house?
   Through the…
   a. Window b. Roof c. Floor d. Door

2. People at the pool of Bethseda were healed when…
   a. A clock struck b. A priest came
   c. Thunder roared
   d. An angel stirred the water

3. Who was beheaded?
   a. James b. Peter
   c. Mary d. John the Baptist

4. What did Jesus say when the disciples stopped the children from seeing him?
   a. Thank you b. Do not stop them
   c. I'm too tired d. Nothing

5. What did Jesus do before his last meal to teach his friends to serve one another?
   a. Prayed
   b. Washed his disciples' feet
   c. Sang d. Set the table

6. Jesus said Peter would deny knowing him three times before he heard …
   a. A dog bark b. A bell ring
   c. A gun fire d. A cock crow

7. In whose tomb was Jesus buried?
   a. Joseph of Arimathea's
   b. Simon of Cyrene's
   c. Peter's d. Herod's

8. Which of these men did Jesus take with him into Gethsemane?
   a. Stephen b. James c. Paul d. Luke

9. Who thought Jesus was a gardener when he rose from the tomb?
   a. Peter b. Thomas
   c. A Roman guard
   d. Mary Magdalene

10. Where was Jesus when he rose into heaven?
    a. Mount of Olives/Bethany
    b. Galilee c. The Temple
    d. Mount of Beatitudes

Answers to be found on page 102

Jesus' last week

1. On the Sunday before he died, Jesus came into the city on a donkey. What did he do when he saw the city?
   a. Wept b. Laughed
   c. Shouted d. Prayed

2. In the week before he died, Jesus drove out the money-changers from the Temple court. True or false?

3. Which disciple did not want Jesus to wash his feet?
   a. Philip b. Peter c. John d. James

4. Which disciple did Jesus send with Peter to prepare the Passover?
   a. John b. Judas
   c. Andrew d. Matthew

5. After Jesus' crucifixion, who asked Pilate for Jesus' body?
   a. Simon of Cyrene
   b. Joseph of Arimathea
   c. Mary of Magdala d. Nicodemus

6. "Golgotha", the place of Jesus' crucifixion, means:
   a. Potter's field b. Tree of Shadows
   c. Hill of Sorrows d. Place of the Skull

7. Whose ear was cut off and then healed in Gethsemane?
   a. Archippus b. Zenas
   c. Malchus d. Aristarchus

8. After Jesus' arrest, who swore he didn't know Jesus?
   a. Judas b. Peter c. Barrabas d. John

9. On Jesus' last night, what did his friends do when he was praying?
   a. Ate a meal b. Sang hymns
   c. Slept d. Talked

10. What did the Roman soldiers put on Jesus' head?
    a. A wreath of laurel leaves
    b. A crown of thorns
    c. A Roman helmet d. A veil

Answers to be found on page 103

Betrayed

1. How many pieces of silver was Judas given to betray Jesus?
   a. 20 b. 30 c. 50 d. 100

2. What did Jesus give Judas as a sign that he was going to betray him?
   a. Glass of wine b. Bread
   c. Jar of honey d. Bag of coins

3. How did Judas show the guards who Jesus was?
   a. Pointed b. Talked with him
   c. Held him d. Kissed him

4. Where did Judas betray Jesus?
   a. Sea of Galilee b. Mount of Olives
   c. Garden of Gethsemane d. Temple

5. What was Judas' particular job among the apostles?
   a. Cook b. Treasurer
   c. Letter-writer d. Publicity

6. Judas helped himself to the disciples' money.
   True or false?

7. The chief priests went secretly to Judas and asked him to betray Jesus.
   True or false?

8. Judas said, "I have sinned for I have betrayed innocent blood."
   True or false?

9. When did Judas go off to fetch the soldiers?
   a. 9 a.m. b. Midday
   c. 6 p.m. d. After it was dark

10. Judas killed himself.
    True or false?

Answers to be found on page 103

Jesus' arrest and trial

1. How many people came to arrest Jesus?
    a. A large crowd **b.** 2 people
    c. A legion **d.** 12 soldiers

2. Who was the chief priest who had Jesus arrested?
    a. Annas **b.** Caiaphas
    c. Moses **d.** Samuel

3. On what charge did the Jewish court sentence Jesus to death?
    a. Murder **b.** Theft
    c. Drunkenness **d.** Blasphemy

4. Who was the prisoner the people wanted released instead of Jesus?
    a. Barnabas **b.** Barabbas
    c. Bar-Jesus c. Cornelius

5. Who was told to carry Jesus' cross for him?
    a. Joseph of Arimathea
    b. Simon of Cyrene
    c. Peter **d.** Samson

6. Where was Jesus crucified?
    a. The Mount of Olives **b.** Golgotha
    c. Bethlehem **d.** Mount Carmel

7. What did they offer Jesus to drink as he was crucified?
    a. Water **b.** Wine **c.** Milk
    d. Wine mixed with gall

8. With which former enemy did Pilate become friends as a result of Jesus' arrest?
    a. Annas **b.** Caiaphas
    c. Herod **d.** Judas

9. How many hours of darkness were there when Jesus hung on the cross?
    a. 2 **b.** 12 **c.** 3 **d.** 24

10. How many soldiers crucified Jesus?
    a. 2 **b.** 3 **c.** 4 **d.** 5

Answers to be found on page 103

The first Easter

1. Who told the women Jesus was not in the tomb, but had risen?
   a. The guards b. An angel
   c. Peter d. God in a dream

2. To whom did Jesus first appear after his resurrection?
   a. Mary Magdalene
   b. His mother Mary c. Peter d. Paul

3. What happened to Jesus forty days after his resurrection?
   a. He ascended into heaven
   b. He vanished c. He went to Galilee
   d. He walked to Emmaus

4. Who said he wouldn't believe Jesus had risen unless he could see his nail marks?
   a. Andrew b. James
   c. Peter d. Thomas

5. Where did Jesus talk with Cleopas after the resurrection?
   a. Jerusalem b. Mount of Olives
   c. Road to Emmaus d. Galilee

6. Whom did Jesus tell to "feed my sheep"?
   a. John b. Peter c. Mark d. Paul

7. The last time the disciples saw Jesus, where did he tell them to stay?
   a. Bethany b. Jerusalem
   c. Galilee d. Bethlehem

8. To prove he was not a ghost Jesus ate some...
   a. Bread b. Fish c. Figs d. Meat

9. On Easter Sunday morning, who saw the angel roll back the stone and sit on it?
   a. Mary Magdalene
   b. The Roman guards
   c. Peter d. John

10. On the evening of Easter Sunday, Jesus came to his disciples and said, "... be with you."
    a. Love b. God c. Joy d. Peace

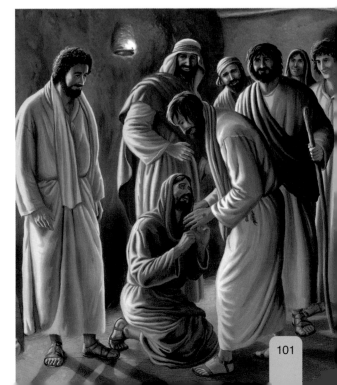

Answers to be found on page 103

The Christmas quiz

1. Bethlehem (Luke 2:4)
2. Mary (Luke 1:27)
3. Bands of cloth (Luke 2:7)
4. In a manger (Luke 2:7)
5. An angel told them (Luke 2:10–11)
6. Returned, glorifying and praising God (Luke 2:20)
7. They saw a star rising (Matthew 2:2)
8. Gold, frankincense, and myrrh (Matthew 2:11)
9. King Herod intended to search and destroy Jesus (Matthew 2:13)
10. Until the death of Herod (Matthew 2:15)

The Jesus quiz part 1

1. At the Temple in Jerusalem (Luke 2:22–24)
2. Nazareth (Luke 2:51)
3. The Temple in Jerusalem (Luke 2:41–50)
4. Carpenter (Mark 6:3)
5. James and John (Mark 1:19)
6. Three (Luke 4:1–12)
7. Nothing (Luke 4:1–2)
8. By the Sea of Galilee (Mark 1:16)
9. Parables
10. About 30 (Luke 3:23)

Miracles

1. 6 (John 2:6)
2. They went into a herd of pigs (Mark 5:11–13)
3. 1 (Luke 17:15)
4. Trees (Mark 8:24)
5. Jesus' cloak (Matthew 9:20–21)
6. His mat (Mark 2:11)

7. The wind and waves (Mark 4:39
8. Cast their nets on the right side of the boat (John 21:6)
9. It was the Sabbath (Luke 13:10–17)
10. The centurion had such great faith (Matthew 8:5–13)

The Jesus quiz part 2

1. God with us (Matthew 1:23)
2. Jordan (Matthew 3:13)
3. Nicodemus (John 3:1–2)
4. Capernaum (Matthew 4:13)
5. "This is my beloved Son" (Matthew 3:17)
6. Passover (Luke 2:41–42)
7. Simon (Luke 7:36, 40)
8. Zacchaeus (Luke 19:1–5)
9. Pharisees (Matthew 12:24, 34)
10. Peter (Matthew 16:23)

Gospel queries

1. Good shepherd (John 10:1–18)
2. Bethesda (John 5:1–9)
3. John the Baptist (John 1:6)
4. Nicodemus (John 3:1–21)
5. Jacob's (John 4:6)
6. Healing of ten lepers (Luke 17:11–19)
7. Pool of Siloam (John 9:7)
8 Governor (Matthew 27:2)
9. Washed his hands (Matthew 27:24)
10. Torn in two (Matthew 27:51)

More Gospel stories

1. Roof
2. An angel stirred the water (John 5:3–7)
3. John the Baptist (Matthew 14:10)
4. Do not stop them (Mark 10:14)

5. Washed his disciples' feet (John13:1–17)
6. A cock crow (John 13:38)
7. Joseph of Arimathea's (Matthew 27:57–60)
8. James (Mark 14:33)
9. Mary Magdalene (John 20:1, 15)
10. Mount of Olives/Bethany (Acts –12; Luke 24:50)

Jesus' last week

1. Wept (Luke 19:41)
2. True (Mark 11:15–16)
3. Peter (John 13:8)
4. John (Luke 22:8)
5. Joseph of Arimathea (Mark 15:42–43)
6. Place of the Skull (Matthew 27:33)
7. Malchus (John 18:10)
8. Peter (Mark 14:66–72)
9. Slept (Mark 14:37–41)
10. A crown of thorns (Mark 15:17)

Betrayed

1. 30 (Matthew 27:3)
2. Bread (John 13:26)
3. Kissed him (Matthew 26:49)
4. Garden of Gethsemane (Matthew 26:36–50)
5. Treasurer (John 12:6)
6. True (John 12:6)
7. False: Judas volunteered (Mark 14:10)
8. True (Matthew 27:4)
9. After it was dark (John 13:30)
10. True (Matthew 27:5)

Jesus' arrest and trial

1. A large crowd (Matthew 26:47)
2. Caiaphas (Matthew 26:57)
3. Blasphemy (John 19:7)
4. Barabbas (Matthew 27:15–26)
5. Simon of Cyrene (Matthew 27:32)
6. Golgotha (Matthew 27:33–35)
7. Wine mixed with gall (Matthew 27:34)
8. Herod (Luke 23:12)
9. 3 (Luke 23:44)
10. 4 (John 19:23)

The first Easter

1. An angel (Matthew 28:5–6)
2. Mary Magdalene (Mark 16:9)
3. He ascended into heaven (Acts 1:3, 9–11)
4. Thomas (John 20:24–28)
5. Road to Emmaus (Luke 24:13, 18)
6. Peter (John 21:17)
7. Jerusalem (Luke 24:49)
8. Fish (Luke 24:42–43)
9. The Roman guards (Matthew 28:2–4)
10. Peace (John 20:19)

Sermon on the Mount

1. What word is missing? "An eye for an eye, and a...for a... "?
   a. Hand **b.** Shoe **c.** Nail **d.** Tooth

2. Jesus said that false prophets look mild, but are really ferocious...
   a. Dragons **b.** Lions
   c. Wolves **d.** Bears

3. Jesus said, "Your Father in heaven looks after the... and will look after you."
   a. Birds **b.** Bees
   c. Wild animals **d.** Butterflies

4. If people hear and do what Jesus tells them, Jesus says they are like a wise man who built his house on a rock. True or false?

5. The Sermon on the Mount can be found in which book?
   a. Matthew **b.** Mark **c.** Luke **d.** John

6. Jesus said, "You are the... of the earth."
   a. Strength **b.** Power
   c. Salt **d.** Foundation

7. Where did Jesus say people should lay up their treasures?
   a. In a bank **b.** In a house
   c. In heaven **d.** In a safe place

8. What is the prayer Jesus taught called?
   a. The Jesus Prayer **b.** God's Prayer
   c. The Long Prayer
   d. The Lord's Prayer

9. What did Jesus tell people not to hide?
   a. Money **b.** Treasure
   c. Light **d.** Leaves

10. Jesus said if someone makes you go one mile, go with them... miles.
    a. Five **b.** Ten **c.** Two **d.** One

Answers to be found on page 112

Jesus' parables

1. What happened to the man who had a bumper crop?
    a. He built bigger barns b. He sold the farm
    c. He gave to the poor d. He gave a party

2. What happened to the weeds that grew up
    in the wheat? They were...
    a. Ground up with the wheat
    b. Cast into the sea c. Burned up d. Abandoned

3. What did the man find in a field, so that he
    sold all he had to buy that field?
    a. A pearl b. A gold chest
    c. Treasure d. A bag of coins

4. Why did the man knock on his friend's door at midnight?
    a. He was ill b. To ask for bread c. He'd been robbed
    d. He could smell smoke

5. How many bridesmaids didn't have enough lamp oil?
    a. 15 b. 7 c. 12 d. 5

6. The man who received five talents from his master earned how many more?
    a. 2 b. 5 c. 100 d. 7

7. Which seed is the smallest, but becomes the greatest garden plant?
    a. Fig b. Pomegranate c. Sycamore d. Mustard

8. Who did the persistent widow keep coming to see?
    a. Doctor b. Teacher c. Judge d. Priest

9. Why was one of the guests thrown out of the wedding party?
    a. He was drunk c. He was greedy c. He wasn't invited
    d. He was wearing the wrong clothes

10. How many coins did the woman have before she lost one?
    a. 10 b. 11 c. 20 d. 99

Answers to be found
on page 112

The Good Samaritan

1. Who asked Jesus, "Who is my neighbour?"
   a. Pharisee b. Scribe
   c. Lawyer d. Priest

2. Where did Samaritans come from?
   a Sumer b. Samaria
   c. Sumatra d. Somalia

3. The story of the Good Samaritan tells of a journey from Jerusalem to where?
   a. Emmaus b. Hebron
   c. Joppa d. Jericho

4. The man was stripped, wounded, and left half dead by...
   a. Policemen b. Priests
   c. Thieves d. Samaritans

5. Who was the first to pass by on the other side of the road?
   a. Samaritan b. Priest
   c. Levite d. Pharisee

6. Who was the second to pass by on the other side of the road?
   a. Samaritan b. Priest
   c. Levite d. Pharisee

7. How many people passed without helping before the Samaritan came along?
   a. 1 b. 2. c. 3 d. 4

8. What did the Good Samaritan do first for the wounded man?
   a. Prayed b. Preached to him
   c. Baptized him
   d. Bound up his wounds

9. Where did the Good Samaritan take the wounded man?
   a. Home c. To a synagogue
   c. To an inn d. To a doctor

10. The Samaritan was:
    a. Walking b. Riding a donkey
    c. Riding a camel d. In a chariot

Answers to be found on page 112

The Prodigal Son

1. How many sons did the prodigal son's father have?
    a. 1 b. 2 c. 7 d. 12

2. Which son asked his father for his share?
    a. Younger b. Middle
    c. Older d. The Bible doesn't say

3. What happened in the country where the prodigal son went?
    a. Flood b. Famine c. Plague d. War

4. When the prodigal son spent all his money, what job did he get?
    a. Mending cars b. Tending sheep
    c. Feeding swine d. Fishing

5. What did the prodigal son eat?
    a. Rotten meat b. Grass
    c. Corn husks d. Burgers

6. On his return home, he planned to ask his father...
    a. For more money
    b. If he could be a servant
    c. For a bath d. For a party

7. Which of the following did the father not give the prodigal son on his return?
    a. Robe b. Ring
    c. Gold and silver d. Sandals

8. Where was the prodigal son's brother when the prodigal son returned?
    a. In another country
    b. In the synagogue
    c. In the field d. In bed

9. What was the brother's response to the celebration?
    a. Joyful b. Angry c. Afraid
    d. The Bible doesn't say

10. What did the father order for the feast?
    a. Boiled pork
    b. Roasted lamb
    c. Fattened calf
    d. Spicy chicken

Answers to be found on page 112

Who asked Jesus?

1. Whose mother asked Jesus to grant her sons places at his right and left, in his kingdom?
   a. Peter and Andrew
   b. James and John c. Jacob and Esau
   d. Priscilla and Aquila

2. Who asked, "How can a man be born when he is old?"
   a. Peter b. Simeon
   c. Abraham d. Nicodemus

3. Which disciple asked Jesus who would betray him?
   a. Judas b. Peter c. John d. James

4. Who asked Jesus, "What shall I do to inherit eternal life?"
   a. Pharisee b. Scribe c. Peter d. Lawyer

5. Who asked Jesus, "Are you the Christ, the Son of the Blessed One"?
   a. Peter b. John c. Caiaphas d. Annas

6. Who asked Jesus how often he should forgive his brother?
   a. John b. James c. Peter d. Andrew

7. Who asked Jesus, "Are you the king of the Jews?"
   a. Pharisees b. Pilate c. Caiaphas d. Herod

8. Which disciple asked Jesus, "How can we know the way?"
   a. Peter b. Philip c. Judas d. Thomas

9. Which disciple asked Jesus, "Teach us to pray... "?
   a. Peter b. Matthew c. John d. The Bible doesn't say

10. Who asked Jesus to remember him when he came into his kingdom?
    a. Stephen b. Paul c. Dying thief d. Peter

Answers to be found on page 112

Jesus the Master

1. When did Jesus say, "I have food to eat that you know nothing about"?

2. What did Jesus offer the Samaritan woman?

3. To which group of people did Jesus say, "God is not the God of the dead but of the living"?

4. From which book did Jesus read at the Nazareth synagogue?

5. Why did Jesus say put oil on your hair and wash your face?

6. Complete this beatitude: "Blessed are the peacemakers for... "

7. What tree did Jesus cause to wither?

8. How many baskets of leftover food were there when Jesus fed the 4,000?

9. What are the miracles always called in John's Gospel?

10. What did Jesus say he did not know?

Answers to be found on page 112

Jesus said...

1. Jesus said people would recognize his followers by what?
   a. Their love b. Their good works
   c. Their faith d. Their wisdom

2. Jesus said that it's more difficult for a rich man to enter the kingdom of heaven than for a camel to:
   a. Fly b. Have triplets c. Speak
   d. Go through the eye of a needle

3. Why did Jesus say to Peter, "Go to the lake and throw out your line"?
   a. He was hungry
   b. He was teaching Peter to fish
   c. Jesus' sandal had fallen into the lake
   d. To find money with which to pay the Temple tax

4. Of whom did Jesus say, "I have not found such great faith"?
   a. The Syro-Phoenician woman
   b. A Roman centurion
   c. Jarius d. Pilate

5. What did the Pharisees do when Jesus said, "Before Abraham was, I am"?
   a. Cheered b. Arrested him
   c. Proclaimed him king
   d. Tried to kill him

6. What did Jesus say is the greatest commandment?
   a. Love the Lord your God
   b. Love yourself
   c. Love other people
   d. Keep the Sabbath

7. Jesus said he came to call... to repent.
   a. Sinners b. Priests c. Jews d. Israel

8. In John's Gospel, how many descriptions does Jesus give of himself which begin with "I am"?
   a. 3 b. 5 c. 7 d. 9

9. To whom did Jesus say, "Everything is possible for one who believes"?
   a. Martha b. The disciples
   c. The father with the epileptic son
   d. Jairus

10. Jesus said he was the true...
    a. Vine b. Apple c. Jew d. Bread

Answers to be found on page 113

Jesus' words

Complete the sentences that Jesus said:

1. No one comes to the Father except through…

2. Ask and it will be… to you.

3. Seek and you will…

4. Whoever wants to be first must be… of all.

5. Those who humble themselves will be…

6. Love your enemies and pray for those who… you.

7. The harvest is plentiful but the… are few.

8. I have told you these things, so that in me you may have…

9. With man this is impossible, but with God all things are…

10. Let the little children come to me, and do not hinder them, for the…
   belongs to such as these.

Answers to
be found on
page 113

Sermon on the Mount

1. Tooth (Matthew 5:38)
2. Wolves (Matthew 7:15)
3. Birds (Matthew 6:26)
4. True (Matthew 7:24–25)
5. Matthew (Matthew 5:1–7:29)
6. Salt (Matthew 5:13)
7. In heaven (Matthew 6:19–20)
8. The Lord's Prayer
9. Light (Matthew 5:14–16)
10. Two (Matthew 5:41)

Jesus' parables

1. He built bigger barns (Luke 12:18)
2. Burned up (Matthew 13:30)
3. Treasure (Matthew 13:44)
4. To ask for bread (Luke 11:5)
5. 5 (Matthew 25:2–10)
6. 5 (Matthew 25:20)
7. Mustard (Mark 4:31–32)
8. Judge (Luke 18:1–3)
9. He was wearing the wrong clothes (Matthew 22:11–13)
10. 10 (Luke 15:8)

The Good Samaritan

1. Lawyer (Luke 10:25, 29)
2. Samaria
3. Jericho (Luke 10:30)
4. Thieves (Luke 10:30)
5. Priest (Luke 10:31)
6. Levite (Luke 10:32)
7. 2 (Luke 10:30–31)
8. Bound up his wounds (Luke 10:34)
9. To an inn (Luke 10:34)
10. Riding a donkey (Luke 10:34)

The Prodigal Son

1. 2 (Luke 15:11)
2. Younger (Luke 15:12)
3. Famine (Luke 15:14)
4. Feeding swine (Luke 15:15)
5. Corn husks (Luke 15:16)
6. If he could be a servant (Luke 1:17–19)
7. Gold and silver (Luke 15:22)
8. In the field (Luke 15:25)
9. Angry (Luke 15:27–28)
10. Fattened calf (Luke 15:23)

Who asked Jesus?

1. James and John (Matthew 20:20–21)
2. Nicodemus (John 3:4)
3. John (John 13:23–25)
4. Lawyer (Luke 10:25)
5. Caiaphas (Mark 14:61)
6. Peter (Matthew 18:21)
7. Pilate (Mark 15:2)
8. Thomas (John 14:5)
9. The Bible doesn't say (Luke 11:1–2)
10. Dying thief (Luke 23:42)

Jesus the Master

1. After talking to the Samaritan woman (John 4:32)
2. Living water (John 4:10)
3. To the Sadducees (Mark 12:27)
4. Isaiah (Luke 4:16–17)
5. So no one will know you are fasting (Matthew 6:16–18)
6. "... they will be called children of God" (Matthew 5:9)
7. Fig tree (Matthew 21:19)
8. 7 (Mark 8:20)

9.   Signs (e.g. John 2:23)
10. The date of his second coming
     (Mark 13:32)

Jesus said...

1.   Their love (John 13:35)
2.   Go through the eye of a needle
     (Mark 10:24–35)
3.   To find money with which to pay
     the Temple tax (Matthew 17:24–27)
4.   A Roman centurion (Luke 7:9)
5.   Tried to kill him (John 8:58–59)
6.   Love the Lord your God
     (Matthew 22:34–38)
7.   Sinners (Matthew 9:13)
8.   7
9.   The father with the epileptic son
     (Mark 9:23)
10. Vine (John 15:1)

Jesus' words

1.   Me (John 14:6)
2.   Given (Matthew 5:16)
3.   Find (Matthew 5:16)
4.   Slave (Mark 10:44)
5.   Exalted (Matthew 23:12)
6.   Persecute (Matthew 5:44)
7.   Workers (Matthew 9:37)
8.   Peace (John 16:33)
9.   Possible (Matthew 19:26)
10. Kingdom of God (Mark 10:14)

Bible animals

Which creatures do you associate with the following?

1. Elijah
2. Eve
3. Balaam
4. David
5. The triumphal entry of Jesus into Jerusalem
6. Paul's shipwreck on the island of Malta
7. Daniel
8. Isaac
9. Prodigal son
10. Jonah

Answers to be found on page 126

Fish and other creatures

1. When Eliezer set off to find a wife for Rebekah, how many camels did he take loaded with gifts?
   a. 2 b.5 c.10 d. 20

2. Which creature was more crafty than any of the wild animals?
   a. Fox b. Wolf c. Serpent d. Hare

3. In Genesis, on which day were fish created?
   a. 3rd b. 4th c. 5th d. 6th

4. What was Jonah swallowed by?
   a. Blue whale b. Shark
   c. Sperm whale d. None of these

5. What birds landed in the desert wilderness near the Israelites?
   a. Pheasants b. Albatross
   c. Quails d. Sparrows

6. What animals did Saul lose just before he was anointed king?
   a. Goats b. Donkeys
   c. Sheep d. Camels

7. What kind of clothes did John the Baptist wear?
   a. Camel's hair b. Sheep skin
   c. Buffalo hair d. Woven cloth

8. The psalmist says, "As the... pants for streams of water, so my soul pants for you, my God."
   a. Donkey b. Lamb
   c. Deer d. Backpacker

9. On one occasion in the Old Testament an animal is spoken of as a pet. Which animal is it?
   a. Dog b. Lamb c. Lion cub d. Fawn

10. What did Jesus call Herod?
    a. Fox b. Wolf c. Dragon d. Snake

Answers to be found on page 126

115

Meeting with angels

1. Who did the angel Gabriel tell she would have a baby?

2. Who dreamed about a stairway to heaven with angels going up and down?

3. Who did an angel save from being eaten by lions?

4. Finish the angel's message to the shepherds: "You will find the baby lying in a... "

5. The word "angel" means messenger. True or false?

6. At first, only Balaam's donkey saw the angel. True or false?

7. Who were kept out of a garden by cherubim?

8. In the wilderness, who told Jesus that angels would help him?

9. What colour were the clothes of the angel who rolled the stone from the tomb?

10. Who is greater than angels?

Answers to be found on page 126

Angels appear

1. What happened to Zechariah after he met an angel?
   a. He could not see b. He could not speak c. He went mad d. He could not walk

2. Which angel told Mary about her baby?
   a. Simon b. Michael c. Gabriel d. Raphael

3. When the angel rescued Peter in prison, chained between two guards, what was he doing?
   a. Praying b. Sleeping c. Singing hymns d. Preaching

4. For whom did an angel bake bread?
   a. Elijah b. Hagar c. Paul d. Jacob

5. Who was struck by an angel, eaten by worms, and then died?
   a. Ahab b. Pilate c. Herod d. Judas

6. How many angels came to rescue Lot from Sodom?
   a. 1 b. 2 c. 3 d. We don't know

7. When an angel came to see Gideon, what tree did he sit under?
   a. Fig tree b. Sycamore c. Oak d. Palm tree

8. In the Gospels, on how many occasions are we told of angels helping Jesus?
   a. None b. 1 c. 2 d. 3

9. In Acts, when did an angel strengthen Paul?
   a. In prison b. In a storm
   c. On trial d. In a riot

10. In Acts, the angel told Cornelius to send for Peter who was in...
    a. Jerusalem b. Samaria
    c. Joppa d. Caesarea

Answers to be found on page 126

True or false?

1. Elisha was bald.

2. Paul hoped to visit Spain.

3. Hezekiah was a prophet.

4. Sennacherib was king of Israel.

5. Jonathan shot arrows to warn David to hide.

6. Jesus' family were at one time asylum seekers.

7. Absalom's hair was so long it got caught in the trees.

8. Peter baptised Jesus.

9. Enoch lived to 969 years old.

10. David danced when the Ark of the Covenant came to Jerusalem.

Answers to be found on page 126

Signs and signals

1. What was the rainbow a sign of?

2. What did Jacob give Joseph as a sign of his love?

3. When the Israelites were marching around Jericho, what was the signal for them to shout?

4. What was a sign for some shepherds outside Bethlehem?

5. When the wise men left Herod, what was the sign that they were heading the right way?

6. What sign did God give to John the Baptist that Jesus was the "Deliverer"?

7. Who put out a sheep's fleece and asked God to make the fleece wet and the ground dry, as a sign that God would give him victory?

8. After Joshua and the Israelites crossed the Jordan, what did they do as a sign of this miracle?

9. What was Jesus' only sign to the Pharisees?

10. What sign did the dove bring back that the flood had gone?

Answers to be found on page 127

Bible maths

1. Which woman had been married five times?
    a. Eve b. Mary Magdalene
    c. Lot's wife
    d. Woman at the well of Samaria

2. How many times did Jesus tell Peter to forgive?
    a. 70 b. 7 c. 70 x 7 d. Always

3. How many deacons did the early church choose?
    a. 3 b. 5 c. 7 d. 12

4. How many years did Methuselah live?
    a. 969 b. 962 c. 983 d. 978

5. How many sons did Isaac have?
    a. 2 b. 6 c. 12 d. 4

6. How many brothers did David have?
    a. 9 b. 7 c. 5 d. 3

7. How many of the twelve apostles were called James?
    a. 1 b. 2. c. 3 d. 4

8. How many children did Jacob have?
    a. 12 b. 13 c. 11 d. 14

9. How many fish did Peter catch during the miracle after Jesus' resurrection?
    a. 531 b. 135 c. 513 d. 153

10. How many fish were used to feed the 5,000?
    a. 2 b. 3 c. 4 d. 5

Answers to be found on page 127

Numbers

1. How many Gospels are in the Bible?

2. How many disciples did Jesus call?

3. Did Jesus send out his disciples in twos, threes, or fours?

4. How many times did the Israelites march around Jericho on the seventh day?

5. How old was Jesus when he went missing in Jerusalem?

6. How many days did Jesus spend in the desert?

7. God told Noah to take into the ark two of every kind of unclean animal (animals that could not be sacrificed).
   True or false?

8. For how many years did the Israelites wander in the wilderness?

9. For how many days and nights did the rain fall during the flood?

10. How many gates are there in the New Jerusalem?

Answers to be found on page 127

Dreams and visions

1. Who dreamed about a stairway to heaven?

2. Who dreamed about sheaves of corn?

3. Who dreamed about fat cows and skinny cows?

4. Who dreamed that an angel told them not to visit King Herod again?

5. Who dreamed he should take his family to Egypt?

6. Who dreamed he saw a sheet lowered from heaven?

7. Who had a vision of a man from Macedonia begging him to help?

8. Who explained the cup-bearer's dream in prison?

9. Who had a vision of Jesus on the road to Damascus?

10. Who saw Jesus standing at the right hand of God?

Answers to be found on page 60

Deaths and raisings

1. How old was Jairus's daughter when Jesus brought her back to life?
   a. 5 b. 7 c. 10 d. 12

2. How long had Lazarus been in the tomb when Jesus raised him from the dead?
   a. 1 day b. 2 days c. 3 days d. 4 days

3. Whose son did Elijah bring back to life?
   a. The widow of Nain's
   b. The widow of Zarephath's
   c. The Shunammite woman's
   d. Elisha's

4. Who raised Tabitha from the dead?
   a. Paul b. Peter c. Stephen d. Dorcas

5. The widow of Nain begged Jesus to bring her son back to life. True or false?

6. When Herod heard of Jesus' miracles, who did he think might have returned from the dead?
   a. Elijah b. Moses
   c. John the Baptist d. Stephen

7. Where did Paul raise Eutychus from the dead after he fell from a window?
   a. Troas b. Berea c. Philippi d. Assos

8. Who said before he was stoned to death, "I see the Son of Man standing at the right hand of God"?
   a. James b. John
   c. Stephen d. Lazarus

9. Who was carried to heaven in a chariot of fire pulled by horses of fire?
   a. Elijah b. Moses c. Elisha d. Enoch

10. According to Paul, how many Christians saw the risen Jesus at the same time? More than...
    a. 40 b. 500 c. 220 d. 350

Answers to be found on page 127

The eco quiz

1. What did Adam and Eve *not* eat in the Garden of Eden?
   a. Fruit b. Nuts c. Meat d. Herbs

2. After five thousand people had a picnic, what did Jesus ask the people to gather up?
   a. Cups b. Plates c. Bottles
   d. Leftover food

3. According to the Bible, when God finished creating the world, he saw all he had made and it was good. True or false?

4. God said he was concerned about Nineveh because it had many people and also...
   a. Many books b. Much cattle
   c. Much gold d. Many houses

5. When Jesus comes again, what will be set free as well as people?
   a. Angels b. Living creatures
   c. All creation

6. In the New World at the end of time, who will lead the animals?
   a. The king b. A warrior
   c. Jesus d. A little child

7. In Deuteronomy, what were the people told not to destroy when they attacked a city?
   a. Buildings b. Wells
   c. Fruit trees d. Animals

8. What was Adam's job?
   a. Hunter b. Gardener c. Carpenter
   d. Fisherman

9. According to the law of Moses, farmers had to harvest right to the edge of the fields and pick all their fruit from the trees. True or false?

10. Who said that God is a gardener?
    a. Jesus b. The writer of Proverbs
    c. Hosea d. Paul

Answers to be found on page 128

True or false?

1. The book of Jude is in the Old Testament.

2. The Old Testament was written in Hebrew.

3. The book of Revelation was written by Luke.

4. The story of Jesus meeting Zacchaeus is in Luke's Gospel.

5. The calming of the storm is the only miracle to appear in all four Gospels.

6. The book of Hebrews was written by Barnabas.

7. There are 36 books in the New Testament.

8. Matthew's genealogy of Jesus goes back to Abraham.

9. The Dead Sea Scrolls included parts of every book in the Old Testament.

10. Christian monks used a printing press to make a Bible.

Answers to be found on page 128

Bible animals

1. Ravens (1 Kings 17:6)
2. Serpent (Genesis 3:1)
3. Ass (donkey) (Numbers 22:21)
4. Sheep (1 Samuel 16:11)
5. Donkey (Matthew 21:2)
6. Snake (viper) (Acts 28:3)
7. Lions (Daniel 6:16)
8. Ram (Genesis 22:13)
9. Pigs (Luke 15:15)
10. Great fish (Jonah 1:17)

Fish and other creatures

1. 10 (Genesis 24:10)
2. Serpent (Genesis 3:1)
3. 5th (Genesis 1:20–23)
4. None of these, was a great fish (Jonah 1:17)
5. Quails (Exodus 16:13)
6. Donkeys (1 Samuel 9:3)
7. Camel's hair (Mark 1:6)
8. Deer (Psalm 42:1)
9. Lamb (2 Samuel 12:1–3)
10. Fox (Luke 13:32)

Meeting with angels

1. Mary (Luke 1:26–38)
2. Jacob (Genesis 28:10–12)
3. Daniel (Daniel 6:21–22)
4. Manger (Luke 2:12)
5. True
6. True (Numbers 22:21–23)
7. Adam and Eve (Genesis 3:24)
8. Satan (Matthew 4:6)
9. White (Matthew 28:3)
10. Jesus (Hebrews 1:4)

Angels appear

1. He could not speak (Luke 1:19–22)
2. Gabriel (Luke 1:26–31)
3. Sleeping (Acts 12:6)
4. Elijah (1 Kings 19:5–6)
5. Herod (Acts 12:21–23)
6. 2 (Genesis 19:1)
7. Oak (Judges 6:11)
8. 2 (Mark 1:12; Luke 22:43)
9. In a storm (Acts 27:23)
10. Joppa (Acts 10:32)

True or false?

1. True (2 Kings 2:23–24)
2. True (Romans 15:24)
3. False: he was a king (2 Kings 19:1)
4. False: he was king of Assyria (2 Kings 18:13)
5. True (1 Samuel 20:20–22, 37)
6. True (Matthew 1:12–17)
7. True (2 Samuel 18:9)
8. False: John did (Matthew 3:13)
9. False: it was Methuselah (Genesis 5:27)
10. True (2 Samuel 6:14)

Signs and signals

1. God's promise to Noah
   (Genesis 9:14–17)
2. A fabulous coat (Genesis 37:3)
3. A long trumpet blast (Joshua 6:5)
4. A baby in a manger (Luke 2:12)
5. The star reappeared
   (Matthew 2:9–10)
6. The Holy Spirit coming like a dove
   (John 1:32–33)
7. Gideon (Judges 6:36–37)
8. Set up 12 stones from the riverbed
   (Joshua 4:1–8)
9. The sign of Jonah
   (Matthew 12:39–41)
10. An olive leaf (Genesis 8:11)

Bible maths

1. Woman at the well of Samaria
   (John 4:7–18)
2. 70 x 7 (Matthew 18:22): Always is
   also correct because that's the
   meaning of 70 x 7
3. 7 (Acts 6:3)
4. 969 (Genesis 5:27)
5. 2 (Genesis 25:21–26)
6. 7 (1 Samuel 17:12–14)
7. 2 (Matthew 10:2–3)
8. 13: 12 sons and 1 daughter
   (Genesis 34:1; 35:22–26)
9. 153 (John 21:11)
10. 2 (Mark 6:41)

Numbers

1. 4
2. 12 (Matthew 10:1–4)
3. Twos (Mark 6:7)
4. 7 (Joshua 6;15)
5. 12 (Luke 2:42)
6. 40 (Mark 1;13)
7. True (Genesis 7:2)
8. 40 (Deuteronomy 1:3)
9. 40 (Genesis 7:12)
10. 12 (Revelation 21:12)

Dreams and visions

1. Jacob (Genesis 28:12)
2. Joseph (Genesis 37:5–7)
3. Pharaoh (Genesis 41:1–4)
4. The wise men (Matthew 2:12)
5. Joseph (Matthew 2:13)
6. Peter (Acts 10:11)
7. Paul (Acts 16:9)
8. Joseph (Genesis [Close up space
   after colon]13)
9. Saul (Paul) (Acts 9:1–5)
10. Stephen (Acts 7:55)

Deaths and raisings

1. 12 (Mark 5:42)
2. 4 days (John 11:17)
3. The widow of Zarephath's
   (1 Kings 17, 24)
4. Peter (Acts 9:40)
5. False (Luke 7:11–17)
6. John the Baptist (Luke 9:7–9)
7. Troas (Acts 20:6–12)
8. Stephen (Acts 7:56)
9. Elijah (2 Kings 2:11)
10. 500 (1 Corinthians 15:6)

The eco quiz

1. Meat (Genesis 1:29–30)
2. Leftover food (John 6:12)
3. False: it was very good (Genesis 1:31)
4. Much cattle (Jonah 4:11)
5. All creation (Romans 8:21–22)
6. A little child (Isaiah 11:6)
7. Fruit trees (Deuteronomy 20:19)
8. Gardener (Genesis 2:15)
9. False (Leviticus 19:9–10)
10. Jesus (John 15:1)

True or false?

1. False. It is in the New Testament.
2. True
3. False. It was written by John.
4. True
5. False. It is the feeding of the 5,000 (Matthew 14:13–21; Mark 6:30–40; Luke 9:10–17; John 6:1–15)
6. False. Nobody knows.
7. False. There are 27
8. True (Matthew 1:1)
9. True
10. False. Christians monks copied by hand. The first complete printed Bible was produced around 1456.